FAIRY TALES AND THE SOCIAL UNCONSCIOUS

NEW INTERNATIONAL LIBRARY OF GROUP ANALYSIS

Series Editor: Earl Hopper

Other titles in the Series include:

The One and the Many: Relational Psychoanalysis and Group Analysis
    Juan Tubert-Oklander

Listening with the Fourth Ear: Unconscious Dynamics in Analytic Group Psychotherapy
    Leonard Horwitz

Forensic Group Psychotherapy: The Portman Clinic Approach
    edited by John Woods and Andrew Williams
    (joint publication with The Portman Papers)

Nationalism and the Body Politic: Psychoanalysis and the Rise of Ethnocentrism and Xenophobia
    edited by Lene Auestad

The Paradox of Internet Groups: Alone in the Presence of Virtual Others
    Haim Weinberg

The Art of Group Analysis in Organisations: The Use of Intuitive and Experiential Knowledge
    Gerhard Wilke

The World within the Group: Developing Theory for Group Analysis
    Martin Weegman

Developing Nuclear Ideas: Relational Group Psychotherapy
    Richard M. Billow

The Courage of Simplicity: Essential Ideas in the Work of W. R. Bion
    Hanni Biran

Foundations of Group Analysis for the Twenty-First Century
    edited by Jason Maratos

The Social Unconscious in Persons, Groups, and Societies: Volume 2: Mainly Foundation Matrices
    edited by Earl Hopper and Haim Weinberg

Applications of Group Analysis for the Twenty-First Century
    edited by Jason Maratos

On Group Analysis and Beyond: Group Analysis as Meta-theory, Clinical Social Practice, and Art
    Anastassios Koukis

The Linked Self in Psychoanalysis: The Pioneering Work of Enrique Pichon Rivière
    edited by Robert Losso, Lea S. de Setton, and David E. Scharff

Group Analysis in the Land of Milk and Honey
    edited by Robi Friedman and Yael Doron

The Social Unconscious in Persons, Groups, and Societies: Volume 3: The Foundation Matrix Extended and Re-configured
    edited by Earl Hopper and Haim Weinberg

FAIRY TALES AND THE SOCIAL UNCONSCIOUS
The Hidden Language

*Ravit Raufman and
Haim Weinberg*

KARNAC

First published in 2017 by
Karnac Books Ltd
118 Finchley Road, London NW3 5HT

Copyright © 2017 to Ravit Raufman and Haim Weinberg.

The rights of Ravit Raufman and Haim Weinberg to be identified as the authors of this work have been asserted in accordance with §§77 and 78 of the Copyright Design and Patents Act 1988.

All rights reserved. No part of this publication may be reproduced, stored in a retrieval system, or transmitted, in any form or by any means, electronic, mechanical, photocopying, recording, or otherwise, without the prior written permission of the publisher.

British Library Cataloguing in Publication Data

A C.I.P. for this book is available from the British Library

ISBN 978 1 78220 268 4

Edited, designed and produced by The Studio Publishing Services Ltd
www.publishingservicesuk.co.uk
email: studio@publishingservicesuk.co.uk

Printed in Great Britain

www.karnacbooks.com

CONTENTS

ABOUT THE AUTHORS — vii

SERIES EDITOR'S FOREWORD — ix

INTRODUCTION — xiii

CHAPTER ONE
"Giving one's heart" and "speaking from the bottom of the heart": the case of the Jewish mother in Eastern European tales — 1

CHAPTER TWO
"Asked for her hand" and the tales about the handless maiden: how is taking the hand associated with a marriage proposal? — 15

CHAPTER THREE
"Living in her skin": social skin-ego and the maiden who enters others' skins in fairy tales — 37

CHAPTER FOUR
Eyes and envy: reading Grimms' *One-eye, Two-eyes and Three-eyes* and its Jewish parallels — 57

CHAPTER FIVE
"I (do not) see what you mean": the concrete and metaphoric dimensions of blindness in fairy tales and the social mind   83

CHAPTER SIX
"To step into someone's shoes": the tales about Cinderella   95

CHAPTER SEVEN
Fire of lust: passion and greed in fairy tales and the social (un)conscious   111

CHAPTER EIGHT
"To eat a crow" (swallow frogs): a story of decrees and humiliation   123

EPILOGUE   133

NOTES   137

REFERENCES   141

INDEX   155

ABOUT THE AUTHORS

Ravit Raufman, PhD, is a clinical psychologist and group therapist, a senior lecturer and faculty member at the University of Haifa, Israel, member of the American Group Psychotherapy Association, and an editorial board member of the *International Journal of Group Psychotherapy*. Her research deals mostly with psychoanalytical approaches to fairy-tales, the affinity between fairy-tales and dreams, and thought processes in fairy-tales and groups.

Haim Weinberg, is a Californian and Israeli licensed psychologist and group analyst. He is past President of the Northern California Group Psychotherapy Society and the Israeli Association of Group Psychotherapy. A distinguished fellow of the Israeli Association of Group Psychotherapy, he is also a fellow member of the American Group Psychotherapy Association, the International Association of Group Psychotherapy, and member of the Group Analytic Society International. He is the director of an international doctorate program in psychology with an emphasis on group psychotherapy at the Professional School of Psychology, Sacramento, California, where he serves as the academic Vice President.

Ravit and Haim co-authored several articles about fairy tales and the social unconscious, one of them won the 2017 Alonso award in group psychotherapy.

*To my granddaughter, Avigayil,
who loves listening to stories and fairy tales.*

To Dror, Bar, Or and Tal, who share the magic.

*We would like to thank Noa Teich Fire for contributing the picture of
the fossil for the cover.*

SERIES EDITOR'S FOREWORD

The emergence of the paradigms of modern science in the context of industrialisation processes has brought multiple benefits to all of us. However, the attendant secularisation of personal and collective life, and the negation of that which is intangible and invisible, have also brought many losses. The calculation of the balance of benefits and losses is political in nature, and reflects conflicts of interest at a particular historical juncture. Only in retrospect can it be seen that many of the benefits and losses were inadvertent and serendipitous. In any case, we have lost touch with the world of fairies, which, not so far away and long ago, included the New World itself, or perhaps *vice versa*.

Parallel processes have included privileging the mentality of the adult over that of the child and adolescent, the sensibility of European explorers and colonialists over that of people with less sophisticated technology and weaponry, who could, therefore, be enslaved and commodified, and the privileging of urban culture over rural culture, the constructed over the natural, and the cosmopolitan over the local. Romantic countertrends have included the rediscovery and elevation of folk wisdom and folk knowledge. For example, we have learned to appreciate the value of traditional medicaments, and French sociology and history have acknowledged the importance of the study of the poor, the dispossessed, and the marginalized. In modern family therapy, it is accepted that insights into the unconscious dynamics of troubled parental relationships are uttered from the mouths of babes.

It is in this context that I try to understand the modern study of folklore in general and fairy tales in particular. I would like to rediscover the sense of enchantment associated with reading and hearing them. The culturally supported imposition of reason over feeling and sensation structures our epistemologies of the external and internal worlds. This is closely associated with the definition of gender roles and gender inequalities, perhaps especially in the context of the separation of the world of work from the world of domesticity. It is important for men to reclaim their capacities for insight into the realm of the spirit and the emotions, which has been relegated to women and children. Perhaps fairy tales can be considered within the context of sacred knowledge, which would facilitate the involvement of men in this field of inquiry. Perhaps grandparents can have a second chance.

Although Foulkes used the term "primordial" for what he regarded as the basic level of communication in groups, with its implications that, in the classical sense of the term, the collective unconscious was an important object of interest, group analysis has not yet provided a comfortable home for the study of fairy tales and other forms of folklore. Of course, psychoanalysts and analytical psychologists have, from time to time, offered interpretation of the unconscious meanings of fairy tales. Despite the various points of view both within and between these two general theories and perspectives, they are in agreement that the main themes of fairy tales are universal, because they are rooted in the lifecycle and other natural features of the species of Homo sapiens. In other words, they are universal, because they are based on projections that emanate from unconscious mental processes inherent in the human brain and human body.

At least two issues are associated with this approach. The first concerns variations on the basic universal themes of fairy tales, which seem to be related to variations in socio-cultural–political patterns, some of which have, in turn, been explained in terms of developmental delays and even vestiges of times past. The second issue concerns the origins of fairy tales. Their richness and complexity go well beyond the elements of projection and unconscious phantasy. In other words, unconscious phantasy does not satisfactorily explain unconscious fantasy. During the last century, most social and psychological scientists have eschewed the study of "in-the-beginning" phenomena, partly because, no matter how creative various hypotheses about what happened might be, what has come to be regarded as "evidence" is as speculative as the hypotheses which require illustration, if not actual testing. After all, plausibility is not a substitute for refutability. This is true even within the hermeneutic approach. Of course, the issues of variation and of origins are completely interrelated.

We have also become increasingly cautious and skeptical about confusing the study of human collectivities and groupings of various kinds with the study of persons. Our understanding of fusionary processes within human relations has supported the need to distinguish the life of the group from the lives of the members of it, with certain exceptions concerning social trauma and patterns of group regression. Similarly, the development of modern epigenetics has not given birth to presumptive perspectives concerning the possibilities of codification of experience within germ cells, with certain exceptions concerning comparatively rare multivariate and multifactorial biological processes.

There are also exceptions to the neglect of fairy tales in Group Analysis. Einhorn has considered the story of Hansel and Gretel from the point of view of the socio-economic and political circumstances of the family and the society within which this tale was popular. The relationship of children to their parents depends on the availability of resources, and on whether their father is in work. Several group analysts whose professional background is in Jungian Analytical Psychology draw on fairy tales as a way of explaining to their patients, both individually and in groups, that certain conflicts are natural and universal, for example, in connection with phases of lifecycle. Peseschkian has used folktales in order to communicate with refugees and immigrants who do not speak the local language of their new European cities. This has proved especially helpful for women who are suffering somatic symptoms related to their traumatic experiences.

I have used Bible stories in an attempt to make contact with difficult patients who reject interpretations, perhaps out of envy, or perhaps in rebellion against judgmental and domineering fathers. I have learned that any cultural product can be used as a shared "mediating object" from which meaning can be co-constructed. Like a group itself, a fairy tale can be understood without the imposition of knowledge on the less powerful partner by the more powerful partner.

Such exceptions are not only of clinical relevance. They also illustrate the perspective in which the unconscious mind is regarded as, in essence, relational and contextual, or, in other words, as a socially unconscious mind. Still, these exceptions do not pretend to address the topics of social variation as opposed to collective universality: the epigenesis of experience, which, in the case of fairy tales, involves the realization of idiom and the interpenetration of the individual and the collective, the interpersonal and the transpersonal.

It is in the context of scientific and secular professional culture that the authors of this imaginative study of the social unconscious and fairy tales have addressed their project. They have even invited us to reconsider the very term "the social unconscious". Perhaps it is too difficult that one term should contain so many elements and so many nuanced twists of meaning. Most of us have moved on from the polemic against the extreme versions and understandings of the Freudian psychoanalytical perspective as rooted in the body and the species, which, in this sense, is indistinguishable from the assumptions of Jung. Some of us have learned that it is very important not to confuse the personal matrix with the dynamic and foundational matrices, and to attend very carefully to the interconnections among them over time.

The group analysis of fairy tales demands critique and development. It invites associative questioning of topics that, for both good reasons and bad, we have ignored for a very long time. I hope that including this book in the New International Library of Group Analysis will provoke a reconsideration of such topics as the origins and changes in socio-cultural "patterns" or "memes". I am certain that the study of fairy tales can provide insights into the unconscious life of groups and the unconscious life of members of them. However, I am equally certain that one day our current efforts to understand such phenomena will be heard as twenty-first century fairy tales in their own right.

Many of the theoretical issues that are raised in this volume have been explored in greater depth in *The Social Unconscious in Persons, Groups, and Societies* (Hopper & Weinberg, 2011, 2016, 2017). Several chapters have been published as articles in important journals in the UK, the USA, and Israel. Chapter Three, "To enter one's skin", received the 2017 Alonso Award for contribution to the theory of group psychotherapy. I have found that presenting a chapter to a seminar of students and inviting them to discuss a particular tale in the context of personal and socio-cultural experience is an excellent pedagogical tool.

Earl Hopper
Series Editor

INTRODUCTION[1]

Somatic and metaphoric aspects of foundation matrices as expressed in fairy tales of different communities

Personal introduction

When we were children, we had an annual ceremony, in which the children graduating kindergarten and starting first grade dramatized the story about the child who asks the Rabbi to teach him the Torah.

"Say 'Aleph'!"[2] ordered the Rabbi.
"How can I know that this is 'Aleph'?" asked the child.
"Say 'Beth'!"[3] ordered the Rabbi.
"How can I be sure that this is 'Beth'?" asked the child.
The Rabbi grabbed the child's ear and tugged hard. "My ear, my ear!!" yelled the child.
"How can you be sure that this is your ear?" asked the Rabbi.
"What do you mean? Everyone knows that this is my ear", wailed the child.
"And this is exactly how everyone knows that this is 'Aleph' and this is 'Beth'", said the Rabbi.

This story, which used to be performed as a kind of passage rite, revealed the magic world of words and letters (and, indirectly, the power of physical experiences). The Rabbi's way of convincing the child to believe in the truth of the letters entertained us. At the same time, it strengthened our belief in our teachers. The excitement involved in this festive event amplified the celebration related to the learning of the "Aleph-Beth". We could view it as a didactic story, aimed at strengthening our dedication to our studies and our belief in adults' justice. However, this story also reveals some deep meanings regarding the relations between somatic and abstract layers in the conscious and unconscious mind: a somatic, physical sensation was the only thing that could truly convince the young pupil. He could not doubt his sensorial experience. The body was the "real truth". Whereas the symbolic letters required explorations and explanations, the body was unquestionable. Of course, the Rabbi understood this. The link he created between abstract language and the somatic experience was apparently geared towards educating the young pupil. Yet, beyond this, the action also forged deep meanings related to the development of abstract constructions in the human mind, as well as to the exploration of the individual and social unconscious.

Theoretical introduction

Different literary products reveal different relations between concrete and abstract layers in the human mind. Kafka's short story "In the penal colony" describes the final function of an elaborate torture and execution device that inscribes in Gothic letters on the skin of the condemned man the article of the code he has transgressed (1966). In this way, the condemned clearly "senses" the judgment. The words convey their message not only through their abstract meaning, but also by way of a somatic experience, in which the words are embedded within the human body and mind. The death apparatus uses language, but the language can only be understood when it is physically engraved upon the body. Anzieu (1989) views the infernal machine of Kafka as an example of one of the functions of what he calls the skin-ego (a detailed discussion on this concept can be found in Chapter Three of this book)—that of registering tactile sensory traces, sending back a mirror image of reality: "A first form of anxiety related to this function is that of having the surface of one's body marked by shameful and indelible inscriptions emanating from the super-ego" (p. 105). This description causes readers to undergo a palpable experience, located somewhere on the borderline between the somatic and the symbolic.

In many cases, the power of words in literary products lies in its ability to use language in a way that triggers and stimulates non-verbal experiences that go beyond language. The different literary genres use different poetic strategies to achieve this goal, in which words can "touch" the soul and body. Whereas Kafka's story describes a death apparatus in which words touch the body, this book focuses on the unique style in which fairy tales convey their messages. Instead of describing words that touch the body, in many cases they actually show us metaphoric ideas in a concrete manner, using a phenomenon fairly prevalent in fairy tales called realization of idiomatic expression, in which a concrete act in the plot "hides" an idiomatic expression. For example, in the Grimm's tale "The Frog King, or Iron Heinrich" (Grimm no.1), we are told about faithful Heinrich, the king's servant, who had been so saddened by his master's transformation into a frog that he had had to place three iron bands around his heart to keep it from bursting with grief. Instead of telling (in words) that Heinrich's heart was broken, the fairy tale literally shows us, in a concrete manner, that his heart is actually broken and needs to be mended. This plot detail hides an idiomatic expression (a broken heart) and, thus, combines concrete and abstract modes of expression, exemplifying this genre's unique location on the border between the somatic and metaphoric aspects of human experience.

Another example appears in a less widely known Jewish version of the famous fairy tale "Bluebeard", in which a maiden is forced to eat a human heart. This apparently bizarre plot detail can be understood as a realization of the idiom *"to eat one's heart out"*. This reversal enables us to understand an act of regret associated with a guilty conscience. Instead of describing a person who "ate her heart out" (suffers, regrets), the story describes a human being who actually eats a heart. This event appears in the story as a strange, magical, and unexplained detail. Decoding and extracting the linguistic–metaphoric expression from the concrete action sheds light on the possible hidden meaning. Our research shows that this mechanism is fairly common and can illustrate central dilemmas in the relations between the different modes of thinking—the concrete non-verbal and the linguistic symbolic. The chapters of this book are full of such examples. Fairy tales are considered as one of the most ancient, oral, archaic, and fantastic genres of all literary products, part of the earliest attempts made by human beings to describe in words deep and archaic experiences. In their illustrative way, the fairy tales' plots tell us something deep and important about what preoccupies human beings in different eras. They also reveal something about the evolution of human thought processes and the relations between thinking in words, and "thinking" in images. We will elaborate on this idea in the introduction and throughout the book's chapters.

Fairy tales and society

As fairy tales cannot be attributed to any one single author, but, rather, belong to the society or community, we view them as a convenient source of learning about social aspects of the human psyche and experience. Based on previous works that view fairy tales as residing on the border between concrete and symbolic realms (Raufman, 2012) in their attempts to describe in words distant and far-removed experiences identified with primary processes, this book is interested in primary dimensions of the mind and the ways they connect to secondary ones.

As fairy tales are considered a relatively collective, cross-cultural genre, concerning issues that go beyond the mind of the individual, they serve as a good vehicle to explore that part of the mind that people belonging to the same society have in common. We call this part "the social mind", but we should make it clear that the social mind is somehow a metaphoric concept: we do not view society as homologous to the individual, who actually has a mind. Rather, we refer to the shared experience, or the foundation matrix, of a certain society. We should also clarify that by "social mind" we refer to the mind of people from the same society, while by "collective mind" we address the part of the mind that people share universally. This is somewhat similar to the difference between the social and the collective unconscious—the first being a term coined in the field of group analysis and the second taken from Jungian theory.

The extent to which people are both restrained and constrained by the society in which they live is sometimes way beyond what we imagine. It is possible to refer to this phenomenon as "social unconsciousness", not because the material (facts/events) is always unconscious, but, rather, because we are not necessarily aware of the ways and extent of its influence upon us.

Universal and local aspects in folklore, psychoanalysis, and group analysis

In our project, we are looking for several forms of reference in order to use fairy tales as part of our inquiry of the social unconscious from a psychoanalytic, group analytic, and folkloristic point of view. Sometimes, we refer to these explanations as "interpretations", which should not be understood as bearing the meaning of classical, conservative psychoanalytic interpretations, but more as explanations from those different frames of reference. In discussing the principle theoretical difficulties in applying classical psychoanalytic theory to folklore, Dundes (1987a) related to the assumption, explicit or implicit, that the theory is universally applicable (p. 23). Dundes quotes Bastian, who believed that the psychic unity of mankind everywhere produced similar elementary ideas, and Levy-Bruhl, who claimed that the logical structure of the mind is the same in all known human societies (1975, p. 49, cited in Dundes, 1987a, p. 6). Such approaches do not recognize the existence of a national or social unconscious. However, even Freud, who developed his theory along the lines of individual treatment, referring to the unconscious as an individualistic concept, claimed later on, in *Moses and Monotheism* (1939a), that a "national character" can be identified, and posed the idea of ontogenetic recapitulation of phylogeny, which claims that individuals at birth possess a sort of collective social memory as part of the life experience handed down by their forbears.

Foulkes referred to the foundation matrix of a society as "a firm pre-existing community or communion between the members, founded eventually on the fact they are all human" (Foulkes, 1990, p. 212). Thus, some elements of the foundation matrix are based on the social, cultural, and communicational arrangements that are typical of that kind of society: some elements are based on the arrangements of the particular society, and some are based on the species Homo sapiens and, therefore, are likely to be universal (Hopper & Weinberg, 2011, p. xlvii). We follow this idea by first looking at some unconscious aspects of the specific culture in which each fairy tale discussed throughout the book is told and preserved, and then at some more universal aspects, associated with more primary and somatic aspects of human experience, claiming that the phenomenon of realization of idiomatic expressions explored in each chapter could shed light on the connections between the somatic (which is more universal) and the abstract. We do not pretend to provide a detailed analysis of the social unconscious of different ethnic communities mentioned in this book. Such a project is way beyond our scope and ability. Rather, we focus on how fairy tales can teach us something about the social unconscious in general and bring some examples of different versions. Each society and culture discussed in this book deserves a continued research that cannot be done here.

Hopper and Weinberg (2011) also thoroughly discuss the difference between the group analytic concept of the social unconscious, relevant to a specific society, and the Jungian collective unconscious, universal and common to all human beings, although modern Jungians refer to cultural unconscious (Henderson, 1984) and cultural complex (Singer & Kimbles, 2004).

Foulkes (1990) argues that "... even a group of total strangers, being of the same species and more narrowly of the same culture, share a fundamental mental matrix (foundation matrix)" (p. 228). This foundation matrix is the subtract for the social unconscious. Scholz (2014) explains that "The best known elements constituting this foundation matrix is language, but it also includes all kinds of bodily cues" (p. 203). In this book, we suggest different modes of the foundation matrix and social unconscious: symbolic–metaphoric aspects of the social unconscious and the way it is connected to somatic sensorial aspects of the social unconscious.

Idiomatic expressions, fairy tales, and trauma

Based on a psycho-linguistic model that views idiomatic expressions as a bridge between somatic and mental experiences (especially somatic idioms, that is, idiomatic expressions that include body parts, see Raufman & Yigael, 2011), this book explores the phenomenon referred to as realization of somatic idioms, which appears in fairy tales of different ethnic communities, in order to touch upon the relations between the different modes of expression and the way they connect with each other in the social mind.

The unconscious effect of words and their associations, of which we are unaware, on our sensations, body, and behaviour, has attracted the attention of scholars from various disciplines—linguistic, psychoanalysis, and others. In this project we focus on some social aspects of this comprehensive topic.[4]

Developmental research (e.g., Bauer, 2004) describe the preverbal infant's capacity for representing patterns of interaction in the external world before explicit forms of memory begin to function, and before any symbolic description of such interaction is formulated. Although the ability and propensity to learn language and use it in the service of imagination and communication is likely to be innate, both for the human species in general and for individual human beings, at some point of development the meaning of specific words, expressions, and idioms are often repressed and split off. Thus, such processes belong to the dynamic unconscious of individuals (Hopper & Weinberg, 2011), which is completely intertwined with the dynamic social unconscious (meaning the repressed parts of the psyche that people of the same society share in common without being aware of it).

In addition, recent studies (Raufman & Yigael, 2010, 2011) have shown that language might be connected with primary levels of mental organization. Some linguistic expressions are connected with preverbal and even somatic levels of organization and some somatic experiences are embedded in various linguistic phenomena, such as idioms that refer to body parts. This book focuses on such idioms and the way they are realized in fairy tales—a social product perceived as the most universal genre among all folk genres, or, at least, widespread and cross-cultural. Such fairy tales can be viewed as a fundamental element of the foundation matrix.

For a long time we have known that fairy tales have much to tell us about many aspects of human nature, as well as society, culture, political institutions, etc. Some of the important and meaningful material described in this genre reflects issues that consciously preoccupy the people who tell these stories. They use the narratives to design and construct various life situations and to convey messages that sometimes could not be expressed through the formal social channels. Transmitted orally, more degrees of freedom were available to express rebellious or sometimes subversive ideas in comparison to other social products (see, for example, Zipes, 1991). When fairy tales started to appear in print, going through the processes of editing, publishing, and censorship, more complex social dynamics appeared, and some of it is discussed throughout this book. However, alongside realistic aspects reflected in fairy tales (see Holbek, 1998; Röhrich, 1991), many fairy tales reflect and echo far-removed human experiences of which individuals, and society at large, are frequently unconscious (nonconscious and preconscious). It must be acknowledged that what is perceived as "unconscious" often depends on what an observer or discussant has simply failed to recognize. This notion does not contradict the fact that many elements and messages in fairy tales are conscious and intentional.

Historically, it is possible that the symbolic equation appearing in fairy tales could be seen as initial, early attempts to form a narrative of some sort about a primary experience, usually a traumatic one. Therefore, an analysis of such fairy tales is likely to lead to the uncovering and deep understanding of the possible meanings of such tales and their main elements in relation to early human experience, as well as to a better understanding of the ongoing attraction, and even institutionalization, of such stories. Such processes serve to circumvent emotional experience, and might even be elements of encapsulation processes in response to traumatic experiences (Hopper, 2003a). Freud himself (1918b) believed that events or mental experiences that have not gone through symbolization, will be perceived as traumatic, unfamiliar to the mental system, and detached from other experiences. Much later, Ogden (2010) argues that the model of the mind developed by Fairbairn (1952) includes the idea that the formation of the internal object world is always, in part, a response to trauma: "Every infant realistically perceives the limits of his mother's capacity to love him and this realistic perception is 'traumatic'" (p. 110).

We assume that some early traumatic experiences are universal, and find their muffled echo in those hidden somatic idioms that have been realized in fairy tales. There is a strong affinity between failed dependency as the essence of all forms of traumatic experiences and the term "absentation", taken from the study of folktales, coined by the Russian formalist Vladimir Propp (1968). In his morphology of the folktale, Propp analyses the basic components of Russian folktales in order to identify their simplest irreducible narrative elements. He argues that all fairy tales are actually different versions of the same narrative. Other scholars have shown that this morphology can be applied to folk tales of other communities, not only Russian (Ben-Amos 1967; Dundes, 1964). In fact, an important element in fairy tales is that usually they begin with some kind of deficiency, lack, or crisis, which forces the hero (or some other members of his family whom the hero will later need to rescue) to undertake a journey in order to repair this "initial situation" in which one has to leave the security of the home environment (Propp, 1968).

In an attempt to provide a universal explanation of traumatic experiences, Rank (1929) suggested that all human beings suffer trauma by virtue of being born and of the inevitable, violent, physical and psychic separation from our mothers that we suffer at birth. He argues that birth is an interruption of blissful uterine life from which people spend the rest of their lives trying to recover. In a way, all fairy tales reflect such a departure from a blissful, calm, harmonic situation into disequilibrium, as one is forced to leave the security of home/womb and journey into the dangerous, unknown world.[5]

Assumptions about the structure of the foundation matrix

Before we go further, we need first to clarify the structure of the foundation matrix and then describe the relationship between the somatic and the verbal aspects of psychic development.

As mentioned above, communication in a group is possible because all group members, of all groups, are part of a wider social matrix, called the foundation matrix. Several authors include different aspects or dimensions in their description of the foundation matrix. Foulkes mentions the biological aspect through the anatomy and physiology of the species, and includes culture, language, and social class as the main features of this matrix. Le Roy (1994) discusses family systems, gender relations, and relations between the generations as part of this matrix. Dalal (2001) adds the entire social structure, including power relations and history. Scholz (2017) focuses on the time dimension and shows how the foundation matrix slowly changes across generations. However, too often the discussion of the foundation matrix neglects the importance of the human body as carrying meanings. Elias (1994) termed the concept "habitus", which is closely related to the foundation matrix, and Bourdieu (2000) has further developed this concept. Habitus refers to the lifestyle, values, dispositions, and expectations of particular social groups that are acquired through the activities and experiences of everyday life. In other words, the habitus could be understood as a structure of the mind characterized by a set of acquired schemata, sensibilities, dispositions, and taste. The particular contents of the habitus are a complex result of embodying social structures, such as the gender, race, and class discrimination embedded in welfare reforms, that are then reproduced through tastes, preferences, and actions for future embodiment. Habitus means embodied social values and is one's physical and psychological demeanor, a result of habits developed over a period of time. Accordingly, we can easily connect the idea of habitus to the somatic aspects of the social unconscious.

The somatic and the symbolic in psychoanalytical thought

Exploring the realization of idiomatic expressions, with a special emphasis on what we call somatic idioms (idioms that include body parts) is a way to understand the relationship between primary and secondary mental processes and between concrete and abstract modes of thinking (Raufman, 2012); therefore, to learn more about the ways in which somatic aspects of the social mind are connected to higher ones. Some early somatic experiences might be called "sensations", and it is questionable whether or not they can actually be put into words. Previous psychoanalytic authors, including Klein, Tustin, Milner, Ogden, Winnicott, and Lacan, have tended to equate non-verbal forms of mental representation with the preverbal functioning of infancy, implying that these forms cannot be translated into language. We suggest that some verbal expressions can be identified with pre-logical thinking, which recognizes the primary level of mental organization as a pre-linguistic level (Raufman & Yigael, 2011). In other words, some somatic sensorial experiences are, in fact, embedded in language. This notion is supported by findings in the field of neuroscience (Schachter & Moscovitch, 1984), suggesting that implicit forms of representation are fundamental to complex adult functioning as well as to infant functioning. Psychic organization is usually configured in structural terms and understood to be vertical and hierarchical; thus, these terms are depicted in uni-directional linear terms: secondary processes over primary ones, conscious over unconscious, etc. We believe in a non-linear model of psychic organization, where different modes exist side by side.

In the Kleinian tradition, we usually identify two mental positions that accompany human beings throughout life: the schizoid–paranoid position and the depressive position. A thorough study of the deeper undifferentiated levels of the mind reveals another position, starting even earlier in the infant's development: the autistic–contiguous position. According to Ogden (1989), this position is associated with the most primitive mode of attributing meaning to experience. He suggests that these sensory experiences occur outside the range of language, and that only their muffled echoes are reflected in somatic symptoms. Actually, Ogden was not the first to suggest this hypothesis. Bleger (1967) suggests the existence of a third position that interacted with the schizoid–paranoid and the depressive ones. He called it the "glishro-karyc position" and described it in terms of a fully indiscriminate primary fusion between subject and object, mind and body, self and environment (see Tubert-Oklander, 2017). This is where our approach differs from Ogden's conceptualization of an autistic–contiguous position (1989), as a psychological organization/position that is more primary than either the paranoid–schizoid or the depressive position. For Ogden, the autistic–contiguous mode is a sensory dominated, pre-symbolic mode of generating experience. He is clearly talking about a primitive type of mental function, providing the beginnings of a sense of the place where one's experience occurs. We see different modes of the social mind and different levels of mental organization in the foundation matrix as existing side by side. Somatic idioms are the way language connects the highest levels of mental organization to the most primary ones.

From a different perspective, Bion (1967) describes two modes of mentalization involving alpha-type, and beta-type elements. Alpha-type elements are available for thinking, whereas beta-type elements are not. The containing mother translates what is absorbed by the baby through the senses in a preverbal form into words, and the baby gradually learns to translate its experiences from bodily sensations to thoughts and concepts. Beta-type elements are understood as somatic, raw, unprocessed impulses, which virtually circumvent the minds of both infant and mother. We suggest that those realizations of somatic idioms appearing in fairy tales are a kind of social expression (or that part of the mind that people belonging to the same society share in common) of the ongoing shift between "alpha-function" mechanism (for translating somatic, raw materials into metaphors and images, which then become cultural elements) and beta-elements, reviving the primary, non-verbal experiences. These hidden idioms might serve as a bridge between the container that transforms beta-elements into alpha ones, and the archaic bodily feelings linked to the infant's very earliest sensory and relational experiences. Adults effectively lend the child their own "thought-thinking apparatus" to reshape, detoxify, and transform the beta-elements into alpha-elements. Fairy tales can reflect both modes of thinking of adults and infants. We assume that these processes can be found on the social level as well. Biran (2003), following Bion's concepts, shows how difficult it is to transform beta-type elements into alpha-type elements, in the case of two societies in conflict. Fairy tales, frequently told by female adults, might serve as social "alpha functions" and, by realizing somatic idioms, help the listeners/audience to metabolize the archaic sensory aspects of the foundation matrix into thoughts that can actually be expressed, and, at the same time, revive the archaic experience and help it forge its way to language.

Metaphors, idiomatic expressions, and somatisation

The discussion of the affinity between language and body has a long history in psychoanalysis, beginning with Breuer and Freud's work in *Studies on Hysteria* (1895d). They describe the case of a patient with a neural pain between her eyes that was associated with her grandmother's penetrating stare and the thought that her grandmother suspected her of something. The idiomatic expression "a piercing gaze" was converted in this case into somatic symptom (for further reading, see Chapter Four on eyes and envy). McDougall (1998) views somatization as a metaphoric expression of a mental disorder. She describes a case of a patient who had a heart problem as a concrete expression of the idiom "to be heartless" (see Chapter One on the Jewish mother, and for a review of the differences between McDougall and Freud, as well as some other theoreticians, see Raufman & Yigael, 2010).

In his book, *Circular Reflections*, Pines (1998) connects the symbolic function to the ability to put back together or bring back that which has been lost. He mentions that reparation, putting back together and finding the lost object, are implicit in the concept of symbolism. In fact, Kleinian analysts (see Segal, 1957) link this notion to the capacity to achieve the depressive position. We believe that somatic expressions function as a bridge between different levels of mental functioning and thought. The phenomenon of realization of idiomatic expressions in fairy tales demonstrates the ongoing shift between these two modes of thinking. Idioms that include body parts and body actions have the power to evoke the primary level of the mental apparatus, within which language is embedded. Metaphors are not only a type of poetic expression, but, rather, a basic way of thinking and comprehension, rooted within the nervous system (Lakoff & Johnson, 1980). We can identify the somatic basic of this cultural, linguistic phenomenon, which all human beings have in common. As Raufman and Yigael (2011) pointed out, whereas *metaphors* express the experiences of the subject in the world, *somatic idioms* express intersubjective impressions: a heavy heart, a broken heart, turning a blind eye, a penetrating stare, and so forth, are all expressions connecting physical sensations to elements of speech (tongue), feelings (heart), and sight (eye).

Powell (1982) points out that metaphors must be taken into account in their psycholinguistic function as a special kind of verbal "sign". Metaphors are laden with symbolic inferences. He mentions that metaphors are often paradoxically primitive and concrete in their imagery and abstract in their implications: "This is found in remarks like 'I'm not going to swallow that!' An interplay is conjured up between the physical and the psychic, reminiscent of Freud's notion of the ego as primarily a body ego" (p. 131). He also reminds us that group analysis (and group therapy in general) provides us with a setting in which metaphor plays a particularly central role. Indeed, the ability of the group to play with metaphors, idioms, and verbal expressions is a good sign that the group is alive, moving forward, and has a therapeutic potential. However, Powell did not relate specifically to idiomatic expressions and the way they are realized in group analysis, a topic thoroughly addressed in this book.

The relevance to group therapy and social processes

Anzieu (1989), who coined the term "skin-ego", suggests that, similar to the skin, which serves as the body's envelope, the ego/self envelops the psychical apparatus. This concept consists of both concrete and abstract meanings. In another chapter in this book, we demonstrate its relevance to our perspective. Anzieu (1999) applies his skin-ego concept to group therapy. The term "group skin", also coined by him, as well as similar ideas, serve us, as group therapists, to discuss throughout this book the relation between the somatic and the symbolic in the context of group dynamic, group therapy, and society at large, using fairy tales as a source of knowledge. Various group vignettes are analyzed in the light of these ideas.

Politicians and the media use somatic images to describe a nation, knowing the extent to which people react to such an image on a primary level. For example, the term "body of the nation" illustrates how national identity is experienced as if it has a body (see Weiss, 2002). The same image is used in the USA to describe the war over United States' borders, and the need to monitor internal intruders (Martin, 1990). Another use of this term occurs in nationalism. In its extreme version, nationalism represents a collective dream about territory or masses of people constituting bodies politic. In nationalism, the self is relocated. The central fantasy of nationalism is the creation of an immortal body through elimination of the "enemy" (Koenigsberg, 1996).

Musolff (2010) believes in the powerful impact of metaphors about social groups to misrepresent reality for large masses of people. It could make them literally "see" the referent of the metaphor as belonging to a different social class and act according to this misrepresentation. The metaphor with which Musolff is concerned is that of the body politic—the reference to a political community as an organic body. Identification with a body politic implies escape from one's own body into the "body" of the nation (Koenigsberg, 1996). The totalitarian fantasy is that nothing exists separately from the omnipotent organism: Many human beings are united into one body and people are as cells of an enormous body. This is a concrete demonstration of Hopper's massification pole in his fourth basic assumption (2003a). As will be demonstrated, some fairy tales express this idea.

The organism metaphor, comparing society to a body, has a tremendous power to shape reality and is specifically used for the denigration of marginalized groups in a certain society, wherein the target group is portrayed as a threat to the integrity of the "social body". The Nazis in general, and Hitler's *Mein Kampf* in particular, applied it successfully to a Germany attacked by "parasites"—Jews. Such an image, crystallizing stereotypes of those groups as inferior and dangerous, is extremely powerful, as it is addressing the primary somatic dimension of the social unconscious of the people from that society. It is possible that people belonging to the same foundation matrix experience similar unconscious sensory and somatic aspects, and that certain idioms evoke these experiences in them.

The local and the cross-cultural in fairy tales

The human body is more universal than other (un)conscious elements (such as cultural ones). Thus, expressions related to body parts and bodily actions can reflect more universal issues. In each of the tales presented in this book, one can identify aspects of a specific society, both conscious and unconscious (for example, fairy tales told by Moroccan Jews that might reflect their situation under a foreign regime), and also collective unconscious aspects (for example, the way the heart is used to describe emotions). Whereas societies differ from one another in many cultural, social, and linguistic aspects, the somatic, primary level of experience is a more common area. This deep sensorial level operates in similar ways among people throughout the world. However, in different societies they may attain different forms. Fairy tales are good examples of illustrating the crossroads at which the local meets the more universal. The realization of somatic idioms creates a bridge, linking the concrete and the symbolic. We can say that, although all human beings experience similar sensory and somatic sensations, they can become aware of them in different ways and attribute specific meanings to them within the context of the foundation matrices of their particular societies and other social groups.

In other words, in regard to the individual, idioms and word coinages bridge the two modes of thought processes, which various psychoanalytic schools discuss under different names (primary processes *vs.* secondary ones, alpha and beta functions, etc.). Similarly, the use of somatic idioms in fairy tales bridges the same modes of experience in the social mind: Along with the effort to examine the realization of idiomatic expressions in tales told in different languages, it should be kept in mind that a large part of the phenomenon is quite universal and does not depend on a certain language or culture. This part of the phenomenon relates to the human body and somatic experiences, and is universal, echoing the distant and early experiences of humanity. The individual is exposed to these somatic–sensorial experiences at birth, before being inaugurated into culture and language. We should remember that adaptation processes of folk-tales in general, and the changes they undergo during their periods of wandering from one society to another in particular, are very complex. Consequently, many details are dropped, added, elaborated, and transformed along the way. In many cases, it is impossible to trace and identify all the factors involved in shaping the final style of each version. Along with the ongoing explorations of local factors involved in shaping the tales, this book claims that the primary level of mental organization, the one that is governed by somatic sensations and somatic–sensorial experiences, operates in the fairy tale genre in a somewhat cross-cultural manner. Still, each ethnic community shapes and designs its own version, so that a mixture of universal and local influences is evident, reflecting the combination of primary and secondary thought processes expressed in the tales. Relating to Propp's morphology (and in a totally different context), Jason (1977) asserts that the deep level structure of oral narratives is abstract and possibly universal. In contrast, the culturally specific characteristics of a given oral tradition, including their meanings, are present only at the surface level.

Somatic expressions as living fossils

"Living fossils" represent ways of life that have not changed for prolonged periods of time, perhaps eras, in evolutionary terms. These ways of life have been frozen in time. In a way, the experiences often described in fairy tales operate in a similar way. Despite changes that fairy tales have undergone on the way from being orally transmitted to printed versions, which we have already described, many elements are still preserved today, sometimes in a very similar form to that which was told a long time ago. Fairy tales describe human experiences in verbal language. In fact, they can be perceived as living fossils. Although they use language, they focus on archaic levels of body parts and somatic experiences, attempting to integrate affect, cognition, and behavioral dimensions, but remaining outside the realm of awareness, perhaps as reflected in Bollas's "unthought known" (1987).

Using fairy tales in order to explore the social mind is related to early ideas that viewed fairy tales as retaining traces of an earlier evolutionary stage, when our forbears had not yet advanced very far down the path towards higher individual development (see, for example, Steiner, 1911, cited in Holbek, 1998, p. 227). However, whereas Steiner claimed that our forefathers were much closer to the spiritual world than we are now, and were still possessed of the "atavistic second-sight" which enabled them to perceive, in a certain state of awareness, astral beings and events which are imperceptible to us at our present stage of development, this book suggests viewing fairy tales, or, at least, some of its marvellous elements, as retained traces of the far-off history of the individual or, in other words, as living fossils. The concept of evolution made its way into folk-tale research through anthropology, notably through the writings of Tylor, Lang, Hartland, and a few other British folklorists. In his *Primitive Culture* (1958), Tylor defines primitive features in contemporary European culture as survivals from earlier cultural stages. The folk-tales were viewed as examples of such survivals that could be interpreted to reveal earlier stages in human thought processes. Discussing the phenomenon presented in this book (viewed as a "survival" of primary thought processes of the individual's mind), in the light of Tylor's doctrine of survival (in terms of earlier cultural stages), may remind us of the early observation later adopted by Freud and his followers, suggesting that ontogenesis recapitulates phylogenesis. However, the sense of wonder, which provides the tale with its magical, fantastic nature, is probably related to the archaic nature of the experiences described in fairy tales. These experiences are captured in a verbal–sensorial–behavioral structure, which sometimes lacks the emotional component that connects it to other experiences. Perhaps this structure lacks the ability to describe emotions in a way that is familiar in other genres. The sense of wonder also relates to the question of how much control people feel they have over their environment, especially their natural environment. Recognizing powerlessness in controlling nature is a developmental step, but it is accompanied by turmoil, and sometimes experienced as traumatic. We suggest that the magical, marvelous elements of fairy tales might be connected to the implicit traces of the far-off history of the individual and his social/cultural environment, hence our perception of fairy tales as living fossils.

Each of the chapters in this book presents an example that serves to demonstrate how exploring the phenomenon of the realization of idiomatic expressions in fairy tales sheds light on the somatic dimension of the social mind and the way it paves its way in the foundation matrix of different societies. In each chapter, we usually introduce one fairy tale (or more), decipher the idiomatic expression realized in the plot, explore the possible meanings of that expression for the specific society in which the tale is told, and look for more universal meanings that go beyond that culture. Group therapy vignettes and other cultural products (especially myths) serve to further discuss additional relevant themes related to the foundation matrix. As Israeli–Jewish writers, one main source that served us in our exploration was the Israeli Folklore Archive (IFA), which includes more than 24,000 folk-tales. However, our book does not just focus on the Israeli–Jewish society, but, rather, addresses more general relations between different modes of experience in the foundation matrix.

We wish the readers an experience of both linguistic and sensorial understanding of the ideas presented here, and, similar to that child studying the Torah, actually feel its relevance to the field of group therapy and social mind.

CHAPTER ONE

"Giving one's heart" and "speaking from the bottom of the heart": the case of the Jewish mother in Eastern European tales*

Let us start with an Israeli–Jewish joke: Children in school were asked to compose an essay using the phrase "There is only one Mom". Danny wrote, "I returned home from school and asked Mom what is there to eat. She replied that there are two apples in the refrigerator. I opened the fridge and shouted, 'There is only one, Mom'."

This joke, whose special function in the Jewish–Israeli society will be discussed later, hints at the struggle between society's expectation of acknowledging the centrality of mothers in their sons' lives and the sons' protest against this oppressive exclusiveness. Cumulative psychoanalytic knowledge emphasizes the centrality of the mother figure in the early development of the infant. Usually, this period is considered non-verbal; however, we have already pointed out (Raufman & Yigael, 2011) that language is already embedded in primary levels of mental organization. In this chapter, we present the parallelism between the primary level of mental organization (in which the figure of the mother is central) and the mother–son relationship as

---

* This chapter is based on our paper, Raufman and Weinberg (2016a).

presented in fairy tales. Analyzing fairy tales dealing with the mother–son relationship, we focus on both content and form: the early relationships presented in the tales are in line with the unique form of language used in the narrative, which echoes primary modes of thinking. The realization of two idiomatic expressions that include the word "heart" helps in learning about this mode of experience. As mentioned in our introduction, fairy tales, which are part of the foundation matrix, are located on the border between the abstract and the concrete, and the phenomenon of realization of idiomatic expressions is part of their hidden language. The more universal/somatic aspect of this phenomenon (to which the individual is exposed at birth, before being inaugurated into culture and language) is in an ongoing interaction with the socio-cultural aspect of a specific ethnic community.

In this chapter, we focus on the folk tales' tradition of East-European Jews and how it reflects aspects of mother–son relationships as they function in their foundation matrix.

"The talking heart"

The tale "The talking heart" is recorded in the Israeli Folktale Archive (IFA) and was told by Jews who arrived in Israel from Eastern Europe. Various Jewish versions of this tale are recorded in the archive, all presenting a similar motif, with the following plot: A Jewish man proposes marriage to his beloved. The maiden is willing to marry her beloved suitor, but only on condition that he brings her his mother's heart. Her lover agrees, and takes his mother's heart out of her body. On his way to his lover, carrying his mother's heart, he falls. The heart speaks to the son, despite having been excised from the mother's body. Worried, it asks the son, "Are you hurt? Are you all right?"

Two concrete actions which appear in the tale can be understood as a realization of idiomatic expressions: The mother who gives her heart to her son is the realization of the idiom "to give a heart", and the talking heart is the realization of the idiom "to speak from the heart". Both idioms appear in many languages, as well as in Yiddish, the language spoken among Eastern-European Jews. The metaphorical meaning of these idioms, hidden behind concrete actions in the plot, is in line with the basic idea expressed in the tale, which relates to the particular, unique relationship between a mother and a son. The way of expressing these deep ideas (using concrete actions instead of symbolic verbal expression), which is related to primary thought processes, is also associated with this unique, early, primary relationship between mothers and children. Hence, the theme of a primary, endless mother's love attains an additional meaning by using a mode of expression that combines concrete and abstract layers of consciousness. The idiom "To speak from the bottom of the heart" refers to honesty and is associated with the ability to put deep emotions into words, and, therefore, hints at the relation between somatic and mental–linguistic aspects in the human mind. These idiomatic expressions, which do not appear overtly in the tale, but are, rather, presented as concrete acts, can evoke the deepest, early, primary emotions, as well as somatic experiences emerging from early developmental stages. The choice to express the abstract idea via a concrete act amplifies the physical sensation and the affinity between the somatic and the mental.

Neither the act of taking out the mother's heart nor the ability of the heart to talk is related to ordinary life. In order to understand them we need to take into consideration aspects that do not necessarily appear on the overt plot level of the story. Apparently, the bride-to-be's request expresses jealousy of her future mother-in-law, as she wishes to take the mother's place in her lover's heart. Even though this kind of jealousy might be familiar in families, the expression of it in this specific, extreme, cruel form, which we do not expect to find in reality, requires explanation. Why was this particular strange act chosen, again and again, in different times and versions of this tale? What mode of experience might it reflect?

In contrast to many other fairy tales, the central relationship in the narrative is not between the suitor and his beloved, but, rather, between the son and his mother. This becomes clear at the end of the story, as the bride-to-be is not even mentioned, only the mother, who keeps talking to her son from her heart. We should understand these two mythological acts in the context of the relationship between concrete and abstract modes of experience.

The Jewish mother's self-sacrifice ("To give one's heart")

In daily language, the expression "to give one's heart" is used in order to describe a situation in which we are willing to give everything to someone for whom we care. This is the most total giving, dedicated to the most beloved one. In all of the Jewish versions, the mother does not rebel against the son's request and is willing to give her heart. Her love is portrayed as total and exclusive, and characterizes only a certain type of relationship—the love between a mother and a son.

In contrast to the son, who is ready to replace the mother with his future bride, the mother never stops loving her son and never displaces her love toward him, even after her death. This is an endless, total love, which crosses any border, including the boundary separating life and death. Strong relations between mothers and sons are not unique to Jewish folklore. Similar stereotypes also exist in other cultures (such as the Mediterranean mother, the Pacha Mama in the Inca mythology, and others). However, in this chapter, we focus on the way in which a cross-cultural phenomenon attains a specific form in the Jewish folk tradition, in which the mother is presented as self-sacrificing.

Many of the Jewish versions of this tale were told by the female figures of the families (mothers, grandmothers) who told them to their sons, or grandsons. From this point of view, the tales may be perceived as didactic, aiming to teach the males in the family that nothing compares to mother's love. This is an intricate message, as, along with demonstrating the warm, total love of the mother, the tales warn against vicious brides and hint that the only safe place in the world is the mother. On the overt plot level, the bride is portrayed as bad and evil. However, as most of the story-tellers are mothers, these versions could be exposing and reflecting the potential jealousy of the mother (and not the bride) who fears that a new, young, pretty lady will take her place. The story-tellers use a rhetorical trick by presenting the mother in the story as an innocent, all-good figure who cares only for her son's wellbeing. Her negative feelings are not described on the overt level, but are rather exposed by enacting a narrative technique of portraying the bride's figure as evil and cruel. In contrast to the mother and son, who are presented as innocent and good, the bride is egocentric and manipulative. In order to replace the mother by another love object, some emotional surgery is necessary. Thus, we can view the cruelty characteristic of the primary thought processes expressed in the act of taking out the mother's heart as a metaphor for this surgery. Just as the father's role in the oedipal stage is to help to sever the symbiosis of mother and son, the bride's role later in life is to continue this separation process.

The mother in this tale personifies nourishing, protecting, and threatening aspects of mothering and its reverse aspect—smothering. Idealizations and exaggerations are always included because of primary levels of mental organization that remain, or become reactivated, during later phases of development of psychic life.

An additional complexity of the messages in the tale is related to the mother who is presented as a victim. The relationship between mother and son is not full of joy and happiness. Instead, the main characteristic is the fact that she is happily willing to die for him. This kind of mother might evoke in her son feelings of guilt and regret. When requested by her son to take some rest from work, a typical sentence attributed to the Jewish mother is, "I shall rest in my grave". Her "love" could cause him to feel entrapped and to prevent him from creating new relationships with other women. Still, we should ask why this specific, strange, concrete act was chosen in order to express this idea. We suggest that the answer lies in exploring the relation between concrete and abstract layers of the mind, and by discussing the status of the heart as an internal organ, and the way in which it operates in the linguistic realm with its appearance in an idiomatic expression in a way that might evoke and revive early sensations emerging from a primary developmental phase in life.

Idiomatic expressions that include the word "heart"

Various idiomatic expressions of different languages include the word "heart". Among them we can mention the idioms "broken heart", "eat one's heart out", "a heavy heart", and many others. As mentioned in the Introduction, McDougall brings a clinical example in which she connected a wish of a patient named "Tim" to be heartless to his physical problem with his heart muscle. McDougall referred specifically to different levels of concretization and symbolization related to symptoms (McDougall, 1998). Only after a while, after this patient had suffered from a myocardial infarction, she understood that the idiomatic expression "to be heartless" is not just metaphoric and could carry tragic somatic implications. McDougall views somatizations as a metaphoric expression of a mental disorder, appearing when ordinary mental coping collapses.

In the Jewish versions of the tale "The talking heart", the heart serves precisely these two realms: the concrete and the abstract. On the concrete level, the moment you take a heart out of someone's body, it causes death. However, the way in which the heart keeps functioning, vocalizing the mother's concerns even after her death, demonstrates the use of the heart in the narrative on the metaphoric level. The first concrete act (taking the heart out of the body) is possible in reality (even though very cruel). The second act (the heart keeps talking) is unrealistic and is possible only in the fictional world of fairy tales. The talking heart can be understood as rebelling against the rules of nature and of life and death. It removes any barrier between the living and the dead and, therefore, any barrier that might exist between the mother and her son. In a world of wishful thinking and fantasies, as in the world of fairy tales, this is possible. The mothers telling these stories to their sons use this content to describe how endless and boundless their love is. They also indirectly hint that, no matter what, they would never free their sons.

Mother–son relationships

There is a grain of truth in the mothers' fears that young women will one day take their place. In normal development, sons would indeed separate one day and leave their families in order to build a new family with a new woman. Psychoanalytic literature dealing with mother–child relationships and with the process of separation distinguishes between sons and daughters' development. While daughters' growth and choosing a male partner, as well as the achievement of their gender identity, do not require separation from the mother, achieving a masculine identity necessarily involves cutting the apron strings (a metaphor for the umbilical cord) and distancing from the mother and everything that is identified with feminine qualities.

Chodorow (1978, 1989, 1999) provides a significant contribution to understanding this process. Contrary to the traditional psychoanalytic model, she claims that differences between boys and girls stem not only from the oedipal period, but also from the pre-oedipal experience. She states,

> ... through relation to the mother, women develop a self-in-relation, men a self that denies relatedness ... in most cultures, the earliest identity for all children is feminine, because women are around them ... such identification is more threatening to the boy, because [it is] more basic, than the elements of masculine identification that a little girl later acquires. (Chodorow, 1989, pp. 15, 36)

Chodorow also states that men's way of overcoming the dread of women is by devaluing every feminine aspect in their psyche, including the expression of feelings and relating to others. This description might provide a possible explanation for the longing of both mother and son for the early period of union, since, once the son grows up, he tends to deny his deep connection to the mother. This situation differs for the girl, whose relationship with the mother is not experienced as being threatening; hence, she does not have to separate from her mother in order to achieve gender identity or to fall in love with a man. As Chodorow puts it, "... they [girls] are brought up primarily by women, their socialization is fairly gradual and continuous in most societies, the female role is more accessible and understandable to the child ..." (Chodorow, 1989, p. 40).

Benjamin has helped to advance the exploration of the role of the mother in the developmental process of achieving gender identity. She discusses the conflict involved in the mother–son separation process. She states,

> the boy does not merely disidentify with the mother, he repudiates her and all feminine attributes. The incipient split between the mother as a source of "all goodness" and the father as the principle of individuation is hardened into a polarity in which the mother's goodness is reconceptualized as a seductive threat to autonomy. Thus, a paternal ideal of separation is formed, which, under the current gender arrangement, comes to embody the repudiation of femininity. (Benjamin, 1988, pp. 135–136)

It seems as if traditionally, for Jewish men, this struggle of the son to establish his masculine identity and differentiate from his mother is particularly difficult and clearly reflected in the stereotype of the Jewish mother and the Jewish folktale tradition.

The tales told by the mothers in the family do not ignore this reality. They present a normative situation in respect to the son's preference. The aspect that is not normative is the way by which the events unfold. From this point of view, the expression "to speak from the heart" describes not only honesty, but also the exact place in which the internal realm is salient and governs the situation. Reality is perceived as harsh and unbearable from the point of view of the mother who refuses to let her son go. At the same time, the mother cannot change this reality. The only solution, therefore, is taken from both the unrealistic realm (the heart which continues talking after the mother dies) and the symbolic realm (the functioning of the heart in an idiomatic expression, reflecting very deep emotions). It is possible that the concrete act of the talking heart demonstrates how the affinity between mother and son is, first and foremost, a physical affinity, preceding the development of other complex emotions, such as love. This affinity is created right after the mother becomes pregnant and the baby is an integral part of her body and not a separate entity. Even after birth, the physical component is salient in the mother–son relationship, as she breastfeeds, holds, and cleans her baby. Very often, she experiences her baby as a part of her body long after birth, perhaps throughout her entire life. From this perspective, it is no wonder that, in such an archaic genre as fairy tales, which are characterized by magical and fantastic elements, the mother's love is described in physical terms, as she gives her heart to her son in the most concrete manner. In the same way as the baby experiences the world in somatic terms, so does the mother, while being equipped with what Winnicott calls "primary maternal pre-occupation" (Winnicott, 1957). Even though the mother also has other modes of experience, she shares with her baby primary experiences related to the world of senses and sensations. The son's future bride cannot give him her heart, or take his, as this act is reserved only to the unique relationship between mothers and sons.

We should remember that one of the main distinctions that the individual has to learn is between himself/herself and the mother, which is actually the basis for the differentiation between self and others. Various theoreticians have related to the separation from the mother's body as a critical stage, in which the ability of symbolization is developed. Most of the psychoanalytic approaches assume that the early experiences of the baby consist of "me" and "not me" components. In the early stages of life, the baby perceives himself/herself and the environment as one entity, with no differentiation. The process that leads to the differentiation between me and not me and between fantasy and reality is called in psychoanalysis "symbolization", and it is a central process in mental life. The language is important here, as it creates a mediation space between subject and object. It enables words instead of concrete objects.

In the Jewish versions of the tale "the talking heart", the concrete meaning of the heart and the symbolic meaning of the word "heart" meet in an interesting manner. The relations between abstract and concrete levels are presented in both the thematic level of the tale (as the story deals with the primary mother–son relationship and with the mother's fear of losing her son to another woman) and the poetic level, by using a plot detail which can be understood as a realization of an idiomatic expression familiar to the society in which the story is told, transmitted, and preserved.

The Jewish mother and the question of national character

Several studies of the national character were published in the middle of the twentieth century (e.g., Benedict, 1947; Gooch et al., 1945; Gorer, 1948, 1949), but almost disappeared later and were considered psychological reductionism until recently. Robins (2005) discusses reasons why national stereotypes are inaccurate, as well as broader issues concerning individual and cultural sources of variation in personality. Studies of the German, Dutch, and Danish national character re-emerged at the beginning of the twenty-first century (Kuipers, 2013).

Freud's idea about the Jewish national character was later criticized by Dundes, who suggested, instead, that the Jewish character is a postnatal trait, acquired through the mediation of culture (Dundes, 1975). Nevertheless, whether mediated by culture or emerging out of a national/social character, in many cases folklore may reflect issues with which a certain society is preoccupied, consciously and unconsciously.

Myths of The Great Mother appear in other cultures: in her benevolent form, she is the good mother who feeds her child, the Virgin Mary, the good nourishing Mother Earth, the Motherland, etc.; in the malevolent form, she is the greedy and devouring Mother Earth, the witch who kills children, the *ghoulah* in Arab folklore, the sea that swallows up sailors, and so forth. We already mentioned the myth of the Mediterranean mother, and the Pacha Mama in Inca mythology. For example, in the Italian folktale tradition, mothers are perceived as threatening their son's autonomy and controlling their lives. Pisani (1993) claims that on the deepest level of the foundation matrix of Southern Italy, the archetype of the primordial Great Mother plays an important role. His argument is that dependence on the mother, deeply rooted in the culture of Southern Italy, expresses itself in two ways: fear of separation and of loss and fear of the devouring fusion. Goldberg (2005) reviews devouring mothers in folklore, mentioning that "in several tales of persecuted women . . . a new mother is falsely accused of having eaten her new born child" (p. 230). The mother is the dominant figure in the field of custom, ceremony, and iconographic images, often experienced by the child as omnipotent and overprotective, but also evil and devouring.

The Jewish mother stereotype is common among Jews and non-Jews around the world. In Israel, it is also called "the Polish mother", and in Yiddish (the spoken language of Eastern-European Jews), it is called "Yidishe Mama". The Jewish mother is portrayed in films, jokes, novels, and many other cultural genres which present her as over-protective, embarrassing, dramatic, high maintaining, envious, manipulative in her victim-style, and causing feelings of guilt. This is especially true in her relation to her son when she tends to cross the line between caring and castrating. She finds it hard to enable her son's freedom and autonomy, and when he leaves her she suffers so badly that he feels "he cannot do it to her".

This stereotype is perfectly portrayed in Woody Allen's scene in the film *New York Stories* (1989), where Sheldon's (played by Allen) overly critical mother magically disappears after meeting his *shiksa* (non-Jewish) fiancée, just to reappear, to Sheldon's horror, in the sky over New York City, beginning to annoy Sheldon and his fiancée by constantly talking to strangers about his most embarrassing moments.

Exploring the joke cycle popularized in the USA in the late 1970s and early 1980s about the stereotype of the Jewish American Mother (JAM), Dundes (1985) argued that these jokes reflect the way Jewish Americans feel and cope with their tradition and origins. An ambivalent attitude among American Jews seems to emerge, in which they seek out their roots in order to create a sense of identity, but, at the same time, wish to overcome patterns that might be considered ridiculous and old-fashioned, exposing the oppressed and persecuted aspect of the Jewish people. The characteristics of the JAM in these jokes include such features as being overly solicitous of her children's welfare, being anxious for her daughters to marry well and her sons to become professionals, forcing food down the throats of her children, and her excessive, unending demand for attention, love, and visits from her children. The Jewish Mother is never happier than when she has something to complain about and when she manages to produce guilt feelings in her children. Dundes suggests that the Jewish mother's overprotective nature emerged from the fact that she had to be strong. In Europe, the Jewish father was a weak figure, since he was primarily concerned with religious devotion to God, while the wife, the more practical figure, ran the household (Dundes, 1985, p. 460).

Addressing the question of whether the JAM is strictly a fictional caricature, or whether this stereotype corresponds to actual personality traits, Dundes presents numerous different opinions (1985, p. 466). He quotes Wolfenstein (1963), who shows the transition from the Eastern-European Jewish family to the American Jewish family, and the changing attitudes that had been achieved; the modern American woman wants her children to grow up and be independent, while the "old-world" European woman is overprotective and keeps her children needy. He suggests that Wolfenstein's essay was inspired by earlier research conducted by Ruth Benedict (1949), who compared child-rearing techniques in selected European countries. What Benedict and Wolfenstein suggest is that the Eastern-European Jewish tradition of nurturing did not fit in with American childcare ideals, especially with respect to creating a sense of rugged individualism. Second- or third-generation American Jews felt the need to reject what they considered to be excessive nurturing; this is a possible reason for the JAM stereotype's appearance. Dundes explains,

> Jewish culture overprotects its children and American culture demands and expects upward mobility for all groups. The ideology is expressed in the idealistic egalitarian phrase that "anyone can be president" (except for women, Jews, blacks, etc.). Thus, the Jew who had to struggle just to make ends meet in Eastern and Western Europe found that struggling in the United States could yield much greater material reward. (1985, p. 468)

Grotjahn speaks of the Jewish joke in general as expressing aggression turned inward, combining sadistic attacks with masochistic indulgence (Grotjahn, 1961, p. 184). Ben-Amos related to the "illusion of self-mockery" in Jewish humour, claiming that the phenomenon is more complex, and that the Jewish raconteurs "do not laugh at themselves, but rather ridicule a social group within the Jewish community from which they would like to differentiate themselves" (Ben-Amos, 1973, p. 125). He echoes Naomi and Eli Katz, who concluded that the second-generation American Jew "wished to separate himself sharply from the unassimilated immigrant" (Katz & Katz, 1971, p. 219), and claimed that Jewish humour served as a proper vehicle for this purpose. In contrast, Brandes suggests that assimilated Jews tell such jokes for precisely the opposite reason: to prove their connection with the authentic, real Jews—their parents and grandparents (Brandes, 1983, p. 239). Dundes thinks that both ideas are correct, and that these jokes express genuine ambivalence; by telling these jokes, American Jews succeed in both distancing themselves from, and associating themselves with, the past vestiges of their ethnicity. In this respect, the ongoing process of the separation from the mother can attain in the Jewish tradition a special meaning, as reflected in the Jewish versions of "The talking heart".

It is possible to conclude that the stereotype of the Jewish mother points at the complicated separation processes between the son and his Jewish mother, which are required in order to build a new family. It seems that Benjamin's statement (1988) mentioned above, regarding the mother as a source of "all goodness" as threatening the son's autonomy, is especially relevant to the Jewish culture.

It still remains to speculate as to why the connection between the Jewish mother and her son is more difficult to untangle than in many other cultures. Partly, this stereotype, flourishing in Israel and the USA, represents the need of the new immigrants to rebel against their motherland in order to achieve the longed-for independence and autonomy in their new land. Whether trying to assimilate into the new American culture, with its emphasis on individualism, or to identify with the heroic Israeli myth of the Sabra, who is strong and independent, the umbilical ties should be severed.

We assume that there are deeper roots for this stereotype, originating in the importance traditionally placed by Judaism on the home and the family, and on the role of the mother within that family. Jewish tradition ennobles motherhood and the only role of the mothers in the European *shtetl* (Jewish villages in Eastern Europe) was to take care of their family. This ennoblement was further increased by poverty and hardship of Eastern-European Jews immigrating into the USA, and by survival threats to Jews immigrating to Israel.

In his attempts to identify the basic components that compose the social unconscious, Weinberg (2007) viewed myths as having central place in the foundation matrix. Fairy tales that are told and transmitted from one generation to another are full of components that are part of the foundation matrix. Hopper and Weinberg (2016) identify transgenerational transmission as contributing to the creation of the social unconscious, especially when dealing with oral transition, which expresses issues that cannot be described at a more formal, conscious level. The Jewish versions of the tale "The talking heart" reflect and echo some universal processes relating to the relation between mothers and sons. However, it seems that, in the Jewish culture, this process carries an important meaning that is highly related to the Jewish foundation matrix. The phenomenon of the realization of idiomatic expressions teaches us about the deep connection between the foundation matrix and the somatic–sensory level. This phenomenon could demonstrate the fact that the relation between the Jewish mother and her son exists at a very primary, deep level: The Jewish mother experiences her son as part of her body. Her heart keeps following him in every step he takes. The appearance of the bride and the fear that she will take the mother's place makes the mother develop manipulative ways to keep her son for herself. The narratives about the talking heart express this idea in both a somatic and metaphoric mode of expression.

A group vignette: looking for the "suitable bride"

The uniqueness of mother–son relationships in Jewish tradition is evident in everyday life. As such, it is often manifested in group therapy's discussions. Below is a vignette taken from a therapy group, exemplifying the Jewish mother–son relationship.

> A thirty-two-year-old North American Jewish male entered a therapy group (composed mostly of non-Jewish members), declaring that he does not understand why he cannot find a suitable bride. He explained the difficulty as stemming from the fact that, being a religious Jew, he restricts

his choice to Jewish women observing the tradition, and that there are not many women of this kind in the area. However, the more he told the group about his family, the more it became clear that he has very controlling parents, especially his mother, to whom he reports every act in his life. He moved out of his parents' house two years ago, pushed by his individual therapist, but he still talks on the phone with his mother every day, telling her in detail what he has been doing, and usually being criticized for not doing it right. His mother comes to his apartment once a week, cleaning, organizing his table and room, and complaining about how untidy and disorganized he is.

Whenever he dates a girl, he has to report in detail about the meeting, the girl's appearance, their discussion, etc. His mother usually warns him that he gives himself away too easily, and that he should not speak about himself and his family too much. She usually finds some fault with the girl and advises him not to continue the relationship. Even when he becomes physically involved with the girl, he feels that he has to let his mother know about it.

In response, one group member shared that it is so difficult to feel anger toward mothers, especially when they give their hearts for their beloved sons . . .

Whereas the group member talked about giving the heart on the metaphoric level, the fairy tale, with its unique language, reminds us of the concrete pole of this metaphor, which has a special meaning in human experience and attains a specific form in the folktale tradition of East-European Jews.

CHAPTER TWO

"Asked for her hand" and the tales about the handless maiden: how is taking the hand associated with a marriage proposal?*

> "When men fight with one another and the wife of the one draws near to rescue her husband from the hand of him who is beating him and puts out her hand and seizes him by the private parts, then you shall cut off her hand. Your eye shall have no pity"
>
> (Deuteronomy 25: 11–12)

In daily language, when we say that something gets out of hand, we mean that it gets out of control. In contrast, being heavy-handed means doing something in a strict way, exerting a lot of control. The analogy between hands and control is probably deeply ingrained in human experience, as many other expressions including the word "hands", existing in various languages, refer to situations of *hand*ling/mis*hand*ling things. For example, when we say that something is close at hand, we mean it is nearby or conveniently located:

---

* Some of the ideas presented in this chapter were published in 2014 as: Raufman, R. "Asked for her hand"—the realization of idiomatic expressions in dreams and fairy tales in relational group therapy: whose needs are these anyway? *Group*, *38*(3): 217–228.

we can have it; it is not beyond our reach. In the same vein, when we need help, we might ask someone to give us a hand and we can also hand over things to others. When things are not well organized, we might say that left hand does not know what the right hand is doing, and when there is nothing for us to offer, we are "empty handed". If you are a good hand at something, you do it well, and most desirable is to have the upper hand.

However, hands are also associated with connections and relationships. If people are hand in glove, they have an extremely close relationship. If people go hand in hand, they work together closely. If things go hand in hand, they are associated and go together. We can see the roles hands play in human daily experience regarding both doing things, and connecting to others. So, how should we relate to a fairy tale in which a heroine has both her hands chopped off by either a stranger or a close relative (father/brother)? And how should we explain the fact that this apparently strange narrative, titled "The Maiden without Hands"[6] is actually very prevalent and widespread, appearing in almost every fairy tales' collection around the world?

Following this book's perspective, understanding it as a realization of the idiom "asked for her hand" (common in many languages),[7] or, rather, "took her hand", several fundamental questions arise: first, as the fairy tale provides an illustrative expression for this metaphor, which is extremely cruel, why a marriage proposal is perceived, in so many different languages (and, therefore, different cultures) as something so cruel and possessive? Another question arises regarding the variations in different versions. For example, in versions in which it is the father/brother who chops off the girl's hands, why should he be the one who "takes the maiden's hand"? What does it tell us about the norms, values, and foundation matrices of different societies?

In this chapter, we discuss the realization of the idiomatic expression "asked for her hand" in both fairy tales and dreams, as well as in a broader social context, in which a marriage proposal is associated with the act of taking a maiden's hand. We find these fairy tales to be a valuable source of knowledge regarding the ways in which marriage has been perceived in society, as well as the imbalance of powers between the sexes. We first present the fairy tale itself, with some considerations regarding typology and interpretation. Later, we discuss the realization of this idiomatic expression in various versions of the tale "The Maiden without Hands" in order to touch upon the possible social meanings of this widespread narrative, which includes such an aggressive, cruel, and gruesome act in its plot. Then we present a vignette taken from a group therapy, focusing on its relational aspects.

The tale of the maiden without hands

This tale is a widespread narrative, prevalent around the world in many different versions. Its wide cross-cultural distribution makes it suitable for interpretations and implications that go beyond one specific individual or society. A version of this tale may be found in almost every fairy tale collection of different peoples around the world (see Shenhar, 1987). However, alongside the cross-cultural aspects, comparing versions of different cultures provides a glance at the ways in which the same motifs attain different meanings in different cultures in a manner that probably has something to tell us about the foundation matrices of these cultures and communities.

The synopsis of the popular Grimm version goes as follows.

A poor miller was offered wealth by the devil if the miller gave him what stood behind the mill. Thinking that it was an apple tree, the miller agreed, but it was his daughter. When three years had passed, the devil appeared, but the girl had kept herself sinless and her hands clean, and the devil was unable to take her. The devil threatened to take the father if he did not chop off the girl's hands, and she let him do so, but she wept on her arms' stumps, and they were so clean that the devil could not take her, so he had to give her up.

She set out into the world, wandered, and was finally found by a king who married her and made new hands out of silver for her. She gave birth to a son, and the king's mother sent news to the king, who had gone off to battle, but the messenger stopped along the way, and the devil got at the letter, altering it to say that she had given birth to a changeling. The king wrote back that they should care for the queen none the less, but the devil got at that letter too, and once again changed it, saying that they should kill the queen and the child and keep the queen's heart as proof.

The king's servant despaired, and, to produce the heart, killed a hind and sent the queen and her son out into the world to hide. The queen went into a forest, and an angel brought her to a hut, and helped her nurse her son. When the king finally found her, he questioned her because his wife had silver hands, but she had natural ones. She replied that God had given them back to her. She went away to retrieve her silver hands that had fallen off and returned to show them the king.

The main motif, the cutting off of the hands (classified as motif Q451.1 in the Thompson classification index, 1955–1958), has attained various analytical interpretations. However, whereas in the Grimm version it is the devil who "asks" or, rather, "takes" the daughter's hands, in many other versions, it is her father or brother, a fact that requires an exploration regarding the subject of incest in both tales (fantasy) and society (reality).

The motif of the maiden's dismemberment

Several scholars have recognized the subject of incest in the tale about the maiden without hands, viewing the cutting of the hands as a symbol for intercourse. Whereas incest can be seen as the father's crime, some interpreted it as the daughter's oedipal desires. Dundes suggests, "If it is not the father who wants to marry his daughter but, rather, the daughter who wants to marry her father, then it is appropriate that it is the daughter who is punished for her incestuous wish" (Dundes, 2002, p. 387). This idea is in line with the much earlier suggestion raised by Rank (1912), who discussed the incest theme in medieval literature. Rank suggests that, in a much earlier form of the folk tradition, the daughter was in love with her father, and was punished for her masturbatory desires by mutilation of her hands (p. 348). Some scholars suggest that interpreting the obviously cruel act of cutting the maiden hands when "her hands are clean" as her incestuous wish, and not as a result of her father's lechery, is a form of "blaming the victim" and reminds us of Freud's shift from the real incest events inflicted by fathers to the imagined fantasy of the daughter, due to social norms (Freud, 1896)—a topic that will be further discussed later.[8]

Whereas in some versions, such as in the famous Grimm version, the possible affinity between this act and the subject of incest is only hinted at, in various versions found around the world, the maiden's dismemberment comes when she refuses the sexual advances of her father or her brother. In his review of the various versions of the tale, Dundes mentions various Romanian versions, which are representative: "an emperor who was left a widower, unable to find a wife more beautiful than his daughter resolved to make her his wife. The girl flees, but her father got wind of her intentions and cut off her hands from the wrist" (1987b, p. 60). Various attempts have been made to explain why her hands are the target of her father, or sometimes her brother.[9] Dundes (1987b, p. 61) reviews some of the interpretations aiming to address the question: why the hands?. Among those that he considers "unconvincing", he cites Knedler (1937), who associates the tale with the classical Greek ritual called "Maschalismos" in which murderers allegedly cut off the extremities of their victims. Fenster (1982) suggests castration anxiety as the key. The heroine's hand becomes a phallus, distributed, transferable—both her father's and her own. Then, because her severed hand is to be interpreted as representing a phallus, she must be considered as not just a woman, but a phallic woman. Although sexual explanations have been suggested for this motif, it is still unclear how this specific cruel act of chopping off the hands is associated with incest.

Following the idea that the phenomenon of realization of idiomatic expressions is prevalent in the fairy tale genre and is one way to put into words primary experiences that originally were non-verbal, we suggest understanding the chopped-off hand motif as the fairy tale's way of saying something deep about the way marriage might be perceived in society. The physical act, and the somatic sensation it evokes, tell something about the primary mode of experience in the social mind and foundation matrix. As this fairy tale is common among many different cultural regions, and as this expression also exists in various languages, we suggest that part of this motif's potential meaning is cross-cultural. However, later we examine the more specific and local ways in which it is manifested in certain ethnic communities, thus shifting from the collective to the social unconscious. Dundes points out that this kind of punning play on words is common enough in both dreams and fairy tales. Since the father is after his daughter's hand, he takes it literally. Indeed, later we present a group vignette, in which a dream including a similar theme of chopping off the daughter's hand was brought to the group. However, although calling himself a "Freudian folklorist", Dundes did not link this idea with the more comprehensive Freudian view of the connection between mental ideas, metaphorical idioms, and somatic behaviors.

Dreams in group therapy

A large body of material has already been written about dreams in group psychotherapy (see, for example, Neri et al., 2002; Ulman, 1996). It is impossible to detail here all the rich material written about this topic. Our experience with working with dreams in group therapy includes the responses of the other participants to the dream-telling event (Raufman, 2008) in a way that enables echoing various aspects associated with the dream that might either be accessible to the dream-teller's consciousness, or, as often happens, they might reflect different aspects of which the dreamer is unaware. The participants are invited to share any thoughts, feelings, or associations that emerge in response to the dream. The mechanism of projective identification (Klein, 1946) is often activated, when the member sharing the dream with the group unconsciously entrusts the group with the conflictual material. In this way, the emotional reactions of the group members (including the group therapist) reveal something about the dreamer's mental experience: the group identifies with conflictual material that the dreamer, for various reasons, is not yet capable of owning, and, thus, projects it into the group.

An interesting way of working with dreams in a group is the social dreaming matrix (SDM) developed by Lawrence (1998). Social dreaming concentrates on the dream and not the dreamer. Whereas therapeutic dreaming focuses on the egocentricity of the patient, social dreaming keeps the socio-centric concerns of the participants in mind. In this technique, participants in the group matrix are invited to share dreams and to associate to one's own and others' dreams as they are made available to the matrix so as to make links and find connections. Thus, this methodology allows some access to, and glimpses beyond, the individual unconscious to the social unconscious. We believe that dreams and fairy tales attain similar qualities of being the royal road to the unconscious; however, fairy tales show us more of the road to the social unconscious.

A group therapy vignette

During the course of a group therapy, one of the members brought the following dream: He is at home with his youngest daughter, finding himself cutting his daughter's hand. The dream appeared as somehow detached and bizarre—the member who brought it could not tell what the dream meant to him, and why he brought it to the group. In response, another member raised the association to the fairy tale about the maiden without hands. The association to the fairy tale enabled attaching potential meanings of the dream in the group context, which were unavailable otherwise. This fact became even more interesting, as the group therapist was preoccupied in those days with a research project dealing with dreams and fairy tales: later, we explore how the therapist's inner world was stimulated in response to the dream, activated by the mechanism of projective identification.

The association to the fairy tale "The Maiden without Hands" enables discussion of the relations between the group and the group's conductor and expands the understanding of relational aspects associated with the therapist's own personal needs and the way in which they were activated in the group.

Following analytical ideas that point to the similarities between fairy tales and dreams, it is possible that deciphering the idiom hidden behind the concrete event in both the dream and the fairy tale will enable our understanding of some of the hidden meanings of both things. Freud claimed that

> if we carefully observe from clear instances the ways in which dreamers use fairy tales and the point from which they bring them in, we may also succeed picking up hints which will help interpreting remaining obscuring in the fairy tales themselves. (Freud, 1913d, p. 283)

Having this in mind, we have at our disposal an additional way to interpret the group process that took place in response to the dream content, in a way that was unavailable otherwise.

Whose needs are at the fore?

The chopped-off hand motif, appearing in both the fairy tale and the dream, may be understood not only due to sexual contents, but, rather, to possessive needs, meaning, "You are mine, you belong to me." This idea, which will be discussed in more detail, is of special importance in understanding the group dynamics, especially in respect of the needs aroused in the group's context, and the relations between the group members and the group therapist. In a comprehensive project that analyses fairy tales in order to learn about the human psyche, we have shown that many of the infant's difficulties have developed in response to the penetration and intrusion of the parent's needs/desires/difficulties into the infant's world, which is not protected enough in early developmental stages (Raufman & Yigael, in press). For example, in many cases the opening of the tale presents a parent and children staying at home (mother goat and the seven kids, Little Red Riding Hood and her mother, a miller and his daughter, etc.). It seems that, up until that moment, they had never gone out of their house and had never been separated from one another.

This means the baby has a shared realm with his or her parent, at least in terms of the infant's own perception. Many tales describe the difficulty of identifying the dangers that exist outside the mental organization, those elements that threaten to penetrate it (the wolf, the devil, the witch), as well as the creation of primary and secondary defence mechanisms (the attempts to defend against the wolf). The shared protected realm is broken very early because of the parents' deficiency (Red Riding Hood's grandmother is ill, mother goat has to leave home to search for food, the miller is poor, Hansel and Gretel's parents abandon them, and so forth). Therefore, the children are prematurely exposed to the parent's inner world. This is only part of the analysis of fairy tales. However, at this point, it is enough to present this idea in order to understand a certain aspect of the group process, which is associated with the therapist's own personal needs and the way they penetrate into the group's process.

The therapist's needs

One major question that arises in any therapeutic endeavor, whether individual or group therapy, is how the needs of the therapist manifest within the patient–therapist relationship. Whereas classical approaches began by viewing the therapist as a blank screen, Freud himself changed his perspective in respect of the status of countertransference, acknowledging the existence of subjective experiences of the therapist that penetrate into the analytic dialogue. The view that emphasizes the role of the therapist as a living entity who shares experiences together with the patient has been further developed by intersubjective and object relation theories (see, for example, Joseph, 1985; Racker, 1957, Symington, 1983; Winnicott, 1945, among many others). It is beyond the scope of our discussion to review this important revolution in the field of psychoanalysis, and many other studies have been dedicated to this topic. In the field of group psychoanalysis, it is possible to mention the differences between two major approaches: that of Bion, which views the therapist as less involved in the group dynamic, a "bizarre" and detached observing object, looking at the group from the outside (Bion, 1959, 1962), and that of Foulkes, which views group analysis as "a form of psychotherapy by the group, of the group, including its conductor" (Foulkes, 1964, p. 63). Our discussion adopts a relational perspective to group therapy which emphasizes the way in which the group analyst plays an active role in the group dynamic, activating and being activated by it simultaneously (see, for example, Billow, 2003; Weinberg, 2015), aiming to understand the way in which the group conductor's needs penetrate, unconsciously, into the group process and are enacted in response to unconscious material of the group, involving the mechanism of projective identification. As the therapist's needs could not be acknowledged and discussed overtly (because they were not conscious and also because discussing the therapist's needs has been perceived as illegitimate and, therefore, dangerous), the dream enabled the group to encounter them, and opened a space for the understanding of some important events in the group's dynamic. An important fact that is relevant to the group process was that the group conductor was preoccupied with a project dealing with groups and fairy tales. At the time of leading the group, he was in the middle of writing this current book on the topic. When the dream was presented in the group, he found himself highly involved, reacting much more actively than to other contents brought to the group discussion.

As mentioned above, there is a common social tendency to blame the victim, especially in situations that are so horrific that they are unperceivable, probably due to the deep need (stemming from religious beliefs) to feel that there is justice in the world, and if a person is suffering, probably s/he deserves it. Whereas these ideas carry important implications regarding social aspects in general, let us first consider how they might be relevant to the understanding of the group process.

Identifying the idiomatic expression "asked for her hand" hidden behind the concrete act in which the father himself "takes the hand" of his daughter brings out the issue of forbidden sexual desires and incest. The many oral versions from around the world that present a lecherous father support this idea. However, whereas the tale presents the sexual desire, other explanations attributed to this tale suggest that the problematic relations begin with a daughter who is trapped in her father's world and cannot operate and function independently. The sexual desire is one way to represent the father's own needs, which threaten the ability of the daughter to find her own voice, not necessarily because he is a pervert, but, rather, due to his personal needs penetrating into her world in a way that is premature for her. In the case description of the famous patient Anna O, Breuer explains how her hysterical symptom, in which her hand was paralyzed, is associated with her father's death. Her mental crisis is directly associated with the period in which she had to take care of her sick father and give up her needs (Freud, 1895d, pp. 195–220).

Dundes suggests another possibility: to view the hand being cut off in the context of guilt. It could be the hand of an adolescent girl who might be guilty of masturbatory behavior. If the action of hands initiated the masturbatory fantasy on the part of the young girl in respect of replacing her mother and marrying her father, then the sinning hand could be punished under the rubric of *lex talionis*, which requires that the punishment fits the crime. Dundes further claims that there is some textual evidence that can be adduced in support of the sexual sinning of hands (Dundes, 1987b, p. 62). For example, a legend attached to Pope Leo, among others, reports that as he was celebrating Easter mass, a woman kissed his hand. This had aroused him sexually and shortly thereafter he ordered that the hand that had scandalized him should be cut off. Later, the people complained because he did not celebrate mass as usual. He prayed to the Virgin, who appeared to him and restored the missing hand. Dundes quotes a literary version of the tale, titled "Figlia del re di Dacia", wherein the heroine cuts off her hand on the Virgin's order because her father has thrust her hand into his bosom and into a more dishonourable place.

Relational aspects as manifested in the group in response to the dream

When the dream described above was presented to the group, the participants found it difficult to relate to. Instead, the group therapist reacted with a high level of involvement, in a way that deviated from his regular style. He asked many questions, and encouraged the dream-teller to say more, and it was evident that the dream material activated him emotionally and intellectually. In response, the participant who brought the dream shared information about his relationship with his daughter, expressing feelings of guilt for not being a good-enough father. In spite of the fact that this participant shared personal feelings, no one related to it and a complete silence prevailed in the group.

Only later could another participant share that something strange was happening in the group, even though she could not tell what it was exactly. When asked by the group therapist, she said she noticed that the group therapist did not react as usual. As a result, there was a shift in the group's discussion, which stopped relating to the dream, and was preoccupied with the response and behavior of the group therapist. Several group members joined in and shared the feeling that there was something different about the group therapist's presence, and one even mentioned that there was something threatening about him. The group therapist realized that he was highly involved because of his own interest in working with fairy tales, and he was aware of the fact that his own curiosity made him ask more questions than usual, instead of letting the group do the work. He felt guilty for this behavior, and interpreted it as being self-centered, struggling with narcissistic needs, and failing to oversee a good analytic process. Even though the association of the tale "The Maiden without Hands" was not brought by him, but, rather, by one of the group members, at the moment it was raised he found himself over-invested and no other associations or additional responses were expressed.

Apparently, the group therapist was insightful. His own needs made him react in such a way that a parallel process was evident between father–daughter relationships in the dream and the tale and the therapist–participant relationships in the group. This assumption can be reinforced by the fact that, from the moment the association of the fairy tale was raised and the therapist reacted to it, no other responses were available. It seemed as if the therapist's response silenced other possibilities and reduced the degrees of freedom in the group, cutting off their associations. In a way, this process is parallel to the maiden's hands being cut off by the father. It is possible that, in this context, the group was threatened by the therapist and his power, as he might have represented the symbolic father, with all the castrating features as presented in the tale. However, this is just an assumption that cannot be validated, since the group did not express it overtly.

Nevertheless, assuming that the deviation from his regular style could be a reaction to his needs, as he was used to having many other needs that did not necessarily make him react like this, some other explanations should also be considered. Only later could the group therapist connect his behavior to the intertextual content of the dream and the fairy tale (in which the needs of the father play a central role). Familiarity with the fairy tale about the maiden without hands, along with its various interpretations, was of help in understanding the therapist's behavior as being activated by the fairy tale's content, behaving like the daughter's possessive father.

This tale (as many other fairy tales) is so ingrained in culture that it seems to be part of the shared experience of a group of people belonging to the same social or cultural community. This may serve as an example of one of the diverse functions that fairy tales can serve in group therapy.

As in many other cases, the dream narrative becomes a social event, in which all group members take part (Schlachet, 1995). This understanding helps to shed light upon the processes taking place within the group: It seems that some of the issues with which the group was preoccupied were associated with questions related to the role of the therapist and his ability to contain the group. The group's emotional reactions to the dream (or, more precisely, the lack of emotional reactions and the discussion being centered on the therapist) revealed that these questions preoccupied the group as a whole and not just the member who told the dream. This meant the dominant behavior of the therapist carried a castrating quality, so that the group as a whole, similar to the daughter in the tale, could not behave freely and could not express itself spontaneously. Discussing the relationship between personal issues and more social issues is similar, in a way, to the relationship between dreams and fairy tales. Whereas dreams are considered more private than fairy tales and might reveal issues relevant to the individual, the creation of fairy tales cannot be attributed to any one single author, and they are considered to belong to the folk, or the group. Therefore, they can reflect and echo desires, conflicts, norms, and fears relevant to the society. However, as dreams and fairy tales share some similar characteristics, in some cases (and especially in group contexts) the dream might function as a social event and activate mechanisms that go far beyond the issues that are relevant to the dreamer's private world. Berandt (1968) argued that dreams can express issues that are social in nature, and, as mentioned above, this is the assumption that SDM (Lawrence, 1998) is based upon. Indeed, the dream narrative that was presented to the group activated mechanisms belonging to group dynamics. This idea might help to better understand the processes that took place in the group.

The above example demonstrates the way in which some complicated processes in the group dynamic "search" for their own ways of expressions. The sophisticated, subtle language of the dream and the fairy tale, including the phenomenon of a realization of an idiomatic expression that emphasized its location on the borderline between primary and secondary, concrete and abstract modes of thinking and expression, served as kind of "agents" to the group's unconscious, and enabled encountering some deep meanings that were in the center of the group's process and dynamics. Multi-dimensional aspects of the therapist's behavior revealed themselves. On the one hand, he was enacted in response to unconscious material brought by the group. At the same time, the main question expressed in both the fairy tale and the group process—Whose needs are these?—could be acknowledged as a real situation in the therapist's mind. Awareness of these dynamics enabled the elaboration of relational aspects.

However, alongside the phantasmatic aspects of issues such as incest, possessiveness, and relationships in general, comparing different versions of the fairy tale enables us to learn something about the different ways in which the same tale is being told and perceived in different societies, in a way that is connected to some real sociocultural situations.

Daughters as their fathers' property

The fairy tale reveals a social norm that might still have traces in various societies, especially in collective ones: Daughters are the property of their fathers and later become women who are possessed by their husbands and other males in their extended families. This theme is represented in the tale, as the father seems to have the right to chop off his daughter's hands and is not punished for this gruesome act. The versions and interpretations connecting the hands being cut off by a lecherous father only strengthen the notion that daughters are the property of their fathers, whose needs come first and, therefore, they can do whatever they want with them.

This reminds us of the myth about the Medieval European "lord's right" (French: *droit du seigneur*; Latin: *ius primae noctis*), where feudal lords supposedly had a legal right to have sexual relations with the brides of vassals on their wedding night. Although there is no real evidence of this right being exercised in Medieval Europe, the spread and popularity of this myth probably hints at how the idea of daughters as the possession of their rulers, their fathers or, later, the feudal lord, resides in the foundation matrix.

This idea is hinted at in the Hebrew Bible, as the tenth commandment says: "Thou shalt not covet thy neighbour's house; thou shalt not covet thy neighbour's wife, nor his manservant, nor his maid-servant, nor his ox, nor his ass, nor any thing that is thy neighbour's" (Exodus 20:14). A wife is compared to a house, a servant, an animal, or property. She is mentioned second, after a house. The implication is clear: women are property. The meaning of the word husband (a house owner) reveals this deep idea.

In many eras and in different cultures, even in Western ones, wives were, by law, the property of their husbands. In some of those cultures, especially conservative and collectivistic ones, people were indoctrinated from birth to believe that it was ordained by nature that men must command and women must obey, sometimes using the Bible or other religious scriptures as their inspiration. For example, until the mid-1800s, most North Americans treated the women they married as their property. Women were legally considered the chattel of their husbands, their possession. Any property they might hold before marriage became their husbands' on their wedding day. Women had no legal right to appear in court, to sign contracts, or to do business. Technically, married women had almost no legal identity. Thus, it is not surprising that a marriage proposal in various societies is experienced as taking a maiden's hand (see http://chnm.gmu.edu/courses/omalley/120f02/america/marriage/).

Cultural aspects: fantasy and reality: the case of the Druze versions

If we are to understand the cutting off of hands as a realization of a marriage proposal (as suggested by Dundes), and, therefore, as an incest (whether as the daughter's wishful thinking or the father's crime), examining the phenomenon of incest and the array of powers in the family/society in which these tales are told and preserved might help to shed light on the relations between fantasy and reality expressed in the tales.

Whereas, in the group process, the issue of the father's need could be dealt with on the level of fantasy, in certain patriarchal societies in real life the father's needs take priority over the daughter's basic needs and incest is a real phenomenon, much more frequent than we used to think. We now present Druze versions of the tale, attempting to address the relation between fantasy and reality in these narratives and how they reflect social issues and, at the same time, are parts of the construction of social norms. We assume that the subject of incest and sexual relations/abuse cannot be dealt with separately from the status of women in patriarchal societies. Whereas incest is a taboo in most cultures, in Druze society women who have been subjected to incest are religious outcasts and pay heavy social prices.

The Druze

The Druze is a monotheistic religious community, which emerged during the eleventh century from Islamism. Druze beliefs incorporate several elements from Abrahamic religions, Gnosticism, Neoplatonism, and other philosophies. In Lebanon, Syria, and Israel, the Druze has official recognition as a separate religious community with its own religious court system.

The Druze versions

Fieldwork conducted in the Druze villages in the Galilee in Israel reveals that the tales about the maiden without hands are quite familiar in the Druze folktale tradition. However, as presented in Raufman (in press), although this tale-type is well known and remains as a living oral tradition, it is absent from the printed collections of Israeli

Druze.[10] Is it possible to understand this fact in the light of Herman's notion (1992) regarding the mechanisms of silencing stories about victimized women? In order to address this question, we should explore the relations between fantasy and reality as expressed in fairy tales, as well as the question of whose voice is reflected in these tales.

Jones suggested reading the tales about persecuted heroines with both social and psychological perspectives in mind. His notion that "the tales appear to be offering its audience lessons about the kinds of problems plaguing these relationships (with parents, husbands and children) and about how to act in response to them" and that "these lessons amount to an initiation into the roles and activities typical of and appropriate for the young heroine" (Jones, 1993, p. 23) might also be relevant in discussing the Druze versions. Bacchilega (1993) points out that the innocent persecuted heroine tales, according to Jones' reading, are mirrors that reflect and refract (young) women's images, with both therapeutic and normative effects. The perspective of young girls and that of patriarchy are both activated, as the narratives chart problems and solutions. Jones concludes that the psychological "portrait" of the innocent persecuted heroine, as inscribed within specific narrative and socializing patterns, is the dominant theme of these stories and, to a large extent, authentically represents young women's maturational experiences. We come back to this notion when analyzing the oral versions collected in what is called collective societies.

Sexual abuse in Israeli Druze society

In a previous work (Raufman. in press) the Druze versions of the handless maiden were discussed in light of social reality, in which the phenomenon of women who are subjected to incest is much more frequent than what we use to think. Findings published by the Israeli national center for victims of the crime of sexual abuse report that one in four women has been subjected to rape and one in six women was a victim of incest (see www.1202.org.il/centers-union/info/statistics/union-data). The evaluation is that in Druze society it is even higher but is less reported, not only because of its being a closed society, but due to the fact that Druze women who were subjected to incest are religiously ostracized and pay heavy social prices.

As suggested by Raufman (in press), these findings raise questions regarding the channels of expression and the catharsis of silenced women in society. The Druze female oral tales about the maiden without hands might be perceived in this light, bringing in a more direct manner the woman's distress and, at the same time, promising her a happy ending and a future in a corrected society. This perspective adopts Jones' idea to view the tales as both a social message and a psychological anxiety.

Below is one Druze version of the maiden without hands, told by Ibsitam Perro, a fifty-seven-year-old Druze religious woman living in Daliat-el-Carmel. The tale was recorded by the Druze student, Yara Hir, and its title is "Kotz el Eibra" ("The thorn of a lesson/moral"):

> "Once there was a married man who lived in the same house with both his wife and young sister. One day, the sister drank water and her belly started to swell. The wife noticed and told her husband that his sister was pregnant. Full of rage, he took his sister to the wood, where he chopped off her hands and abandoned her. She cursed him and wished that he would be stabbed by the Thorn of Eibra and she would be the only one who could cure him. She gave birth to a son and a daughter. One day, she wanted to bathe her children, but they fell into the lake. Two doves witnessed this and gave her feathers instead of hands with which she could take care of her children. She than met a man to whom she told her story and he took care of her and her children, providing them with food, shelter, and even taught them the secret of medicine. One day, her curse was fulfilled and no one but her could cure her brother. She recognized him and encouraged him to tell about what he did. He admitted and regretted it. He took his sister to live with him and banished his wife."

Raufman (in press) suggests that what is perceived in the tale as a happy ending is actually the preference for the sister over the wife. The hint of incest appearing in the opening (one might ask how the sister could get pregnant if the only man in the house is her brother) is reinforced in the end, in which instead of marrying a new man, as usually happens in fairy tales, we see a woman who returns to live with her brother, who banishes his wife. This event sheds light on what first appeared as hurting the basis of family honor (becoming pregnant out of wedlock), while local norms and values are combined within a more general motif usually associated with incest (cutting off the hands).

Similar to the dream-telling event in the group vignette presented earlier, here, too, one might ask whose wish it is. Raufman (in press) suggests that there are several ways of understanding this. It is possible to read the tale under the lens of patriarchal order: the feminine messages inserted related (at least on the overt level) to punishment for the injury, but not for the incest. The idea that the incest might also be the wish of the daughter/sister does not contradict the fact that she is the victim of its actual fulfillment (the father/brother are not the ones who will be religiously ostracized and are not at risk of becoming pregnant) and this is true in both options, whether the tale reflects psychological wishes/fears, or social reality.

In discussing the patriarchal order in Druze society, Falah-Faraj (2005), among others, mentions that if the husband is absent, women are ordered to obey their brothers, who controlled them. They are expected to maintain a modest appearance and avoid contacting men outside the family. In the Druze version presented above, the brother suspects that his sister is involved in promiscuity and cuts off her hands—an act which is not impossible in real life. This version reinforces Gilbert's observation (1985) that fairy tales teach us that, in patriarchal marriage, the brother/equal turns into the father/ruler (p. 503). It is possible to read this text in the light of Jones' idea that

> the tales offer some instructions about how society expects females to behave, part of which is drawn from idealized and sexist conceptualizations of women fostered by a male dominated society ... but the tales also apparently provide dramatic representation of the young girl's point of view... (the texts) reflecting different perspectives simultaneously ... include social norms and values ... and personal anxieties. (Jones, 1993, p. 24)

However, taking into consideration the situation of women in some collective patriarchal societies might challenge Jones' idea that

> there simply are not enough unmitigatedly evil family members in the world to justify the wide spread popularity of these characters in the tales.... the fact that children who grow up with perfectly reasonable parents and siblings love these tales suggests that these characterizations are not necessarily drawn literally from real life events and situations. (Jones, 1993, p. 25)

In a society heavily dominated by males, even loving and caring parents cannot always protect their daughters from this social injustice.

Several scholarly investigations have been dedicated to the exploration of how folk literature dealing with murdering women might reflect realistic aspects in Arab societies (see, for example, Miron et al., 2002). For example, oral Palestinian folktales included in Miron's collection present various representations of women: sometimes they are portrayed as those whose destiny depends on male family members' arbitrariness. Some tales present historic events in which women are stronger and break taboos. However, women's ability to break taboos is very limited and is always carried out inside the house while she advises her husband how to behave. Women who deviate from social norms are all murdered. Those who wish to choose their husbands for themselves, against the will of their male family members, are also murdered. Miron points out that this kind of tale ends with the epic law aimed at restoring the balance in the family or society. In the Druze version, poetic justice is achieved by taking revenge on the villains, who are outside the family, and by reasserting that the heroine is innocent. This way, the narrative reassures patriarchal values and no blame is attached to the horrible events that took place inside the family with the act of cutting off the maiden's hands. The tales presented in Miron's collection reflect both the longing for strong, independent women, and, at the same time, how miserable women totally depend on their male family members. The oral versions presented here reflect mainly the helpless maiden whose only way of surviving is by proving her innocence.

Whose voice is expressed in the tales?

Despite the changes in Israeli Druze women's status, in many cases the common norms uphold women's inferiority. Layish (1982) has found that Druze religious laws that order a greater measure of equality for women are not kept in daily practice due to the extended family model, which does not enable equality. Tssab (1998) points out that, since Druze women do not own property, and since they are ordered to live with a male family member, in case of divorce or widowhood they are dependent upon their brothers (Dana, 1998, pp. 119–123). Even though the situation between the brother and sister in the tale about the handless maiden is not unique to Druze society, it might attain an additional meaning in this specific social climate. Tsaab points out that, even though the legal status of Druze women is much better than that of Muslim women in Israel, their social status is much worse. Having this in mind, the Druze versions of the maiden without hands, which are mostly told by women, could express, echo, and reflect this situation.

The "maiden without hands" tale as representing society at large

The tales can be seen as reflecting the state of society in general, regardless of gender differentiations. In an article dealing with the oral tradition of the Druze community in Israel, Raufman (2011) showed how a community preoccupied with issues of identity easily adopts tales dealing with these issues, such as the tale about the wolf and the kids. The article presents the unique status of the Druze in Israel and the way it is reflected in their oral folk tradition. One central feature of Druze experience is that of being subjected to persecution by other communities who share common characteristics with them, such as Muslims. It is possible that a community being persecuted by factors who used to be considered as "family" could easily identify with the figure of the persecuted heroine, especially the maiden without hands. The Druze broke off from Islam during the eleventh century and since then has been subjected to persecution by Muslims (Atashe, 1995; Ben-Dor, 1979; Firro, 2001; Parsons, 2000). In addition, their life in Israel has never been easy. Ben-Dor describes the difficulties which the Druze have had in adjusting to Israeli society: they have adapted well to the Israeli Defence Forces (IDF), but not to society in general (in Atashe, 1995, p. v). He also describes the Druze's feeling of discrimination. Being "betrayed" twice (first by Muslims and later by the state of Israel) could make it easy to identify not only with the innocent persecuted heroine, but also with the double banishment motif. More specifically, the tale about the maiden without hands, who is subjected to persecution by members of her own family, might be perceived, in this perspective, as a metaphor for Druze relations with the Muslims, who used to be considered as "belonging to the same family" and later became hostile (at least in the eyes of the Druze). Parsons has pointed out that, despite the many cultural and religious differences between Druzism and Sunni Islam, Druzism has evolved from Islam and many of the tenets of Druzism have Islamic origins (Parsons, 2000, p. 13). A maiden who was born and raised in a certain family, sharing the same norms, values, and other characteristics, and who, all of a sudden, becomes persecuted by the ones who used to be, or were supposed to be, on her side, may "talk" to the heart of the Druze community.

Carsch refers to the way in which

> Collective representations remind the group of its ideals, thus not only reinforcing the ideals in question, but also promoting the mutual recognition of the reality and potency of the ideas involved, thereby promoting the solidarity of the group. (1968, p. 494)

He further points out that "Members of the group identify with dramatis personae reflecting the ideals of the culture on the basis of perceptions of a 'common quality'" (p. 495). It is possible to view the persecuted heroine as a metaphor for both the persecuted community and the persecuted women within the community—depending on how we read the story, who tells it, and to whom.

Considering Dundes' suggestion of understanding the chopped-off hand motif in the light of the idiom "asked for her hand" raises questions regarding why a marriage proposal in many different societies is expressed, in daily language, as something in which the young bride-to-be loses her hand. Reading the Druze's feminine oral versions of the maiden without hands sheds light on this dark subject.

In this chapter, we traced the idea of the chopped-off hands motif as reflecting a deep theme in the foundation matrix about men's power, which, in many traditions, was manifested as the husband's legal right to "own" his wife and her property, and the right of the father (and brother) to control their daughters (and sisters). Analyzing the group vignette in which a dream about cutting a daughter's hands appeared, we suggested that it can reflect a deep question about whose needs (not necessarily sexual) take priority and that unconsciously, deep inside, society at large still struggles with women's equality.

CHAPTER THREE

"Living in her skin": social skin-ego and the maiden who enters others' skins in fairy tales*

> "Can the Ethiopian change his skin or the leopard his spots?"
>
> (Jeremiah 13:23)

Here, we present a personal memory of one of us: When I was in my twenties, I watched a beautiful French musical film titled *Peau d'Âne* (Donkey Skin) directed by Jacques Demy (1970). The film was adapted by Demy from *Donkey Skin*, a fairy tale about a king who wishes to marry his daughter. I still remember the image of fair Catherine Deneuve, acting as the princess, donning a donkey skin, fleeing her father's kingdom to avoid the incestuous marriage, while in the background the main theme of the film is playing: "Amour, Amour" (Love, Love). The contrast between her beauty and the ugliness of the donkey's head was striking.

It was only years later that I became familiar with the various interpretations of skin change and entering an animal's skin. They related to this change as an expression of deep psychological

---

* This chapter is based on our paper Raufman & Weinberg (2016b).

transformations and identity dilemmas, which a girl escaping her incestuous father is going through. These interpretations, which are presented later, relate to the affinity between skin experiences and deep psychological meanings. However, while watching the musical, I was not bothered by intellectual questions. Rather, I was entrapped by the visual image of a beautiful maiden entering an animal skin, which was so powerful, evoking sensorial reactions. In line with the theoretical perspective presented in this book, it seems as if some deep messages of the fairy tale genre cannot be rendered in the verbal realm, but, rather, operate on various dimensions of human experience—bodily and sensorial. In the context of realization of idiomatic expressions, just as we wonder whether the Ethiopian changes his skin or the leopard his spots, we can ask what happens to a girl entering a skin that is not hers. What are the potential meanings of such an act?

Let us put aside the donkey's skin for a while. We will re-enter it later after discussing the functions of the skin and the realization of idiomatic expressions related to the skin, as they appear in fairy tales.

The skin-ego concept in psychoanalysis

The idiom "Smooth as a baby's bottom"[11] reflects the popular notion of infant's skin: soft, supple, practically flawless and perfect as a newborn skin appears to be. The touch and smell of a baby's skin is one of the most enjoyable sensual experiences for a parent. The cosmetic industry builds on women's yearning to have such a skin. However, the skin does not serve for external appearance only, and is not only directed outside, but has internal functions as well, and thus serves as an intricate seam between our body and the external environment. This experience is so basic and fundamental that it is not surprising that fairy tales make such a wide use of skin's experiences in their plots. As we shall see later, *Donkey Skin* is not the only tale introducing a visual image hiding an idiomatic expression related to the skin.

The biological functions of the skin include barrier, sensory perception, photoprotection, thermoregulation, immune surveillance, hormonal synthesis, and fluid loss prevention. The skin is the body organ in which touch happens, which has wide-ranging physical and emotional benefits for people of all age groups. The skin is of an organic and an imaginary order, both a system for protecting our individuality and a first instrument and site of interaction with others (Anzieu, 1989).

The centrality of skin-related experiences in human development has been broadly acknowledged in psychoanalytic thought. Bick, Ogden, Anzieu, and others emphasized the role of the skin in regulating various stimulations and in providing a feeling of being emotionally surrounded, serving as a type of psychic envelope.

As mentioned in our introduction, Anzieu (1989), who coined the term skin-ego, suggested that, similar to the skin, which serves as the body's envelope, the ego/self envelops the psychical apparatus. This concept consists of both concrete and abstract meanings. The skin-ego designates a mental representation that infants form, based on their experience of their bodies' surface. The physical body is then used to help them picture themselves as the vessel of their mental contents. The skin-ego belongs to the developmental period in which the psychic ego differentiates from the body ego on the practical/operative level, while remaining indistinguishable from it on the level of imagination (figurative level). This idea is strongly connected to the shift from the concrete to the abstract mode of thinking (or from sensorial/preverbal to verbal), emphasized by all analytic approaches as a crucial process in the psychic life. The phenomenon of a realization of idiomatic expressions (in both fairy tales and somatic symptoms) described in this book exemplifies a bidirectional movement between two kinds of processes—turning sensations into representations, and returning the sensorial aspect to the representations that emerge from the somatic sensations. As is further discussed, the skin-ego (which is both concrete and abstract), originally referring to the individual's development, can be applied to the group as well, and, on a wider scale, to society at large. As the social unconscious includes collective memories, anxieties, defenses, associations, and fantasies (according to Weinberg's definition, 2007), common associations related to body and skin typical of a specific culture are part of it and may be expressed in social products such as fairy tales.

Anzieu (1989) suggests that the ego encloses the psychic apparatus, much as the skin encloses the body. The chief functions of the skin are transposed to the level of the skin-ego, and from there to the level of the thinking ego. The functions of the skin-ego are to maintain thoughts, to contain ideas and affects, to provide a protective shield, to register traces of primary communication with the outside world, to manage intersensorial correspondences, to individuate, to support sexual excitation, and to recharge the libido. In brief, the skin-ego is an interface between inside and outside, and is the foundation of the container–contained relationship.

According to Ulnik (2007), the skin is perceived as being related to contact and contagion, a demarcation of individuality, a place of inscription of non-verbal memories, and so on. He also relates to the skin within the context of the relationship with the mother, describing it as a "skin for two". We feel our skin as being intimately our own; at the same time, it is shared through our encounters with others. Skin both separates us from, and connects us to, others. These qualities might hint at why the term skin-ego is so relevant to group experiences, in which the intricate interplay between connection and individuation takes place.

The skin-ego may be understood as either a metaphor or a concrete entity. Does the envelope, for Anzieu, simply represent a convenient image with which to describe the functions and qualities of the ego, or is it a material reality? It seems this is not merely a matter of textual understanding, but, rather, a question dealing with the way in which the body is expressed through language, and *vice versa*: the way in which language "comes alive" in somatic responses and reactions.

This chapter discusses the phenomenon of the realization of a skin-related idiom that appears in fairy tales. Thus, we reveal another form in which the skin plays a unique role in mediating different levels of mental organization. The idiom in English: "living in their skin" (existing in French, Hebrew, and other languages), on which we focus here, is not merely a description of experience. It also evokes the experience of the skin, with its associated primary sensations. The way in which Anzieu relates to the term skin-ego testifies to the centrality he attributes to the sensorial aspect in human experience. The baby is, first and foremost, sensorial; only later do the sensorial experiences gradually become mental processes. The fairy tale, located on the border between verbal and pictorial modes of thinking, helps to shed light on the role of the skin in human experience.

In order to exemplify the unique status of the skin as representing both somatic and abstract layers of experience, we now turn to a fairy tale dealing with issues associated with some of the skin's functions.

To enter one's skin—the tale of the Seven Sisters: the realization of a skin-related idiom

Below is a Yemeni wonder tale, recorded in the Israeli Folktale Archive, in which an idiomatic expression relating to the experience of the skin attains a concrete form.

The Seven Sisters

Once there were seven sisters, whose mother had passed away when they were young. Their father's new wife ordered him to send his daughters away.

The daughters were left alone in the forest. At midnight, they saw a light shining far off in the distance. They decided to follow the light, hoping to warm themselves. The eldest daughter—the first to reach the light, which shone from a house—called out: "Grandma, grandma".

An old lady let her in and told her, "I will give you food and later you will take the coal and go to your sisters."

But, after finishing the dinner, the old lady said, "Now, give me back the food you have eaten, or I will kill you."

Alas, the child could not give the food back and so she was murdered by the old lady and then skinned. The very same thing then happened to the other sisters, each in her turn, except for the youngest sister, who was wiser than her sisters. As she ate the food, she put one bite in her mouth and one bite in her pocket. When the old lady told her to give the food back, the seventh daughter took the food out of her pocket and threw it at the old lady, who was a witch. The witch fell in love with the girl and wanted to raise her as her own daughter. They lived together for some time, but the child sought revenge. The day came soon when she took it: she pushed the witch headfirst into the fireplace, and killed her.

She then put on her sisters' skins, took all the witch's treasures, dressed up as a dog, and later as a poor boy and went away. Still disguised as a poor boy, she reached the hut of a kindly old woman who agreed to take her in and care for her. One day, when the girl was washing her hair in the field, exposing her feminine identity, a prince passed by and fell in love with her. He cut a piece of her hair and kept it. The king ordered the old woman to find the maiden to whom the hair belonged, but she could not find her. One day, when the old woman was washing the "boy's" hair, she suddenly realized that this was the girl the prince was looking for. The prince married the girl and they lived happily ever after.

Our discussion focuses on central acts in the plot, which embrace deep meanings revealed on both concrete and abstract levels. This helps to shed light on the affinity between those layers of the human mind and the social unconscious. One central event is when the youngest daughter *enters* her sisters' skin. After she kills the witch, she finds her sisters' skins, and "gets into them" before she moves on to search for a new place to live. In Hebrew, as well as some other languages spoken by the communities who tell and preserve this tale, the idiom "to enter one's skin" means to identify with someone, to be able to sense things from someone else's point of view in the most deep, primary, sensorial manner. Adopting Anzieu's terminology, it might echo the phantasy of a shared skin.[12] This idiomatic expression attains a concrete form in this tale: By concretely getting into her sisters' skin the youngest girl demonstrates the idea of having a shared skin. Suffering from an early loss, this need was not sufficiently fulfilled and the sense of identity was not achieved. Deciphering the idiom "to enter their skin" out of the concrete action in which she actually gets into their skin enables us to view this act as a reviving of the metaphorical idea of identification. The following actions in the plot show that the girl indeed searches for her identity: first she dresses as a dog, and afterwards as a poor boy, until her true identity is revealed. Her existence in a skin that does not belong to her is described in the tale as both a concrete act, and an abstract idea, related to matters of identity and disguise. Whereas in daily language the idea of "entering someone else's skin" is a metaphor (even though the experience itself is quite real, involving stimulation of the skin), in the fairy tale, the heroine enters her sisters' skins on the most concrete level. Besides viewing this act as an expression of empathy or resonance, it can also be understood as a need for protection.

The question of what kind of skin we live in is crucial in the establishment of the subject's identity. When object-relations are injured or harmed, the feeling of the skin—as containing and providing a safe environment—is also injured. Instead, a skin can simply feel uncomfortably over-stimulating.

According to Anzieu, the main task of the psyche is to turn sensations into representations of the impulses into words, and primary processes into secondary processes. Whereas Anzieu developed a clinical approach aimed at helping to turn sensations into representations, the fairy tale, through its language, regresses the symbolic representations back to the sensorial realm. This reveals something about the evolution of thought processes and its relation to the world of sensations. However, this regression is not total or complete. Once the more developed processes have penetrated into consciousness, they are absorbed and assimilated into the level of sensations. The idiomatic expressions hidden behind concrete plot details in fairy tales exemplify this bidirectional movement. In the above tale, this idea attains a two-fold expression: the entrance of the maiden into her sisters' skins is not merely an act which hides an idiomatic expression associated with identification ("to enter one's skin"), it also demonstrates the double meaning of the skin in itself as a concrete entity and a symbolic concept as well as its function as a border between the somatic and the mental realms. Anzieu attributed the skin with very central functions, such as holding, containing, individuation, distinction between internal and external environments, as well as attachment. All these functions are relevant to better understanding of the tale about the seven sisters, and, hence, to better understanding of the ways in which concrete and somatic modes of experience operate in the social unconscious.

Containing function

In the same way that the skin helps the child represent himself/herself as an "ego", which contains the mental contents through the bodily experience of the skin's surface, so does the maiden in the story concretely use her sisters' skins in order to find her way in the world. This is a concrete use: a somatic symptom emerges from the lack of a containing skin. She lacks the original containing skin, due to the tragic circumstances under which she lost her mother. Only later is the concrete skin transformed into a representative skin.

Skin-ego phases

While Anzieu emphasizes the importance of the sensorial aspect, he pays equal attention to the "thought" (things which we can think about), and views the spoken word as having containing skin qualities. Among the various dimensions that should be included in the social unconscious, Hopper and Weinberg (2011, p. xxxix) related to the role of language and communication systems, which are important "in general, regardless of what is being communicated".

Scholars refer to the fact that the skin-ego is a metaphor for the surface of the skin, reflecting an internalization of the maternal function. The skin-ego evokes the sense of touch but, at the same time, generates the active mobility that creates a point of contact between the subject and part of the self and other. The skin-ego is established by relying on the functions of the skin and on the illusion provided by the mother, in respect of a shared skin between mother and baby. The skin-ego relies on the body in which the impulse is rooted. In the first phase, the impulse attains a body. In the final phase, it attains a name. In between, it attains a place—a room. The above fairy tale exemplifies this idea: first, the maiden wears her sisters' skins. This is her only way to establish a sense of cohesiveness that helps her leave the witch's house and go out on a journey to places unknown. This behavior can be perceived as expressing the idea that the impulse has a somatic origin, connected to early sensorial and mobile experiences. According to Anzieu, only later does the psychic mechanism represent the impulse by "placing it" (in one's imagination) in one of the sensorial organs, one of the "doorways" located on the body's surface. Finally, the language enables inclusion of the impulse in a phantasmatic scenario, which combines both source and destination in a given time and space.

Identification

Anzieu relates to the idiom "to enter one's skin" (or, as he put it, "to get inside the skin of a character", in French: *"faire peau neuve"*—to turn over a new leaf (Anzieu, 1989, p. 13)), to express issues of identification. This is extremely evident in the above tale and is highly related to expressions of the self and ego. The tale describes the way in which communication between two individuals is possible only when both are in contact: meeting concretely on the plot level. This is highly relevant to group experiences. Anzieu clarifies that the skin is more than an "organ"; it is, rather, a component that may comprise various organs. On the somatic level, its anatomic, physiological, and cultural complexity decentralizes the complexity of the ego on the psychic level. This is relevant to the term group skin-ego, which is discussed later.

Mediating and unifying the senses

Anzieu emphasizes the role of the skin as mediating, differentiating, and unifying the various senses. He quotes the psychoanalyst Barrie Biven, who viewed the skin as providing a phantasmatic nucleus for patients suffering from childhood injury and trauma. Biven brings examples taken from folk literature, prose, and the Bible, which exemplify the way in which the skin is perceived as a concrete entity and as a mental representation in social products. For example, the Bible describes Job's suppurating wounds as an expression of his depressive condition. The establishment of the skin-ego meets the need of a narcissistic envelope, which ensures the wellbeing of the psychic mechanism. The term skin-ego serves as an image used by the childish self in the early stages to represent himself as an ego, which contains psychic contents, based on the way in which the child experiences the surface of his body. The sisters in the Yemeni tale suffer from a lack of proper development and proper representations of the self; thus, they seek out alternative "solutions". The establishment of the skin-ego appears during a period in which the mental self separates from the somatic self on the operative level, but remains connected to it on the representative level. According to Anzieu, the symbiotic reunion with the mother is represented in archaic thought by an image in which the child and mother share the same body surface. Separation from the mother is represented by removing this shared skin. In the tale "The Seven Sisters", this removal of the skin attains the most concrete form possible, when the evil witch, who is a substitute mother figure, literally skins the sisters.

Shared skin

The term "shared skin" plays a central role in group therapy. Anzieu relates to the fantasy of shared skin between a baby and its mother. Having in mind Bion's idea that the group can be perceived as a kind of mother (an idea which is reflected in Foulkes' concept, the matrix), we can see how the early fantasy may be revived in a group context. A similar idea is expressed in the fairy tale: The little girl in the above story did not have enough time to enjoy this fantasy. So, she regresses to this early stage in which babies and mothers share the same skin. From this perspective, the plot sheds new light on the idiom "to enter one's skin": here, it is understood not only as the possibility of identifying with someone, but also as a wish to be part of someone else's existence and to deny feelings of separation and loneliness. Understanding the centrality of this experience in a social product such as a fairy tale might help us to shed more light on similar phenomena in group therapy, and the various functions that group members might serve for each other.

Communicative function

Among the five senses, touch is the only sense which has a reflexive structure: when a baby puts his finger on parts of his body, he experiences two complementary sensations: skin on skin—the sensation of being touched and touching, at one and the same time. The child in the tale must attain a skin in which she can live, as her original envelope has been damaged. Anzieu explains that the maternal environment is called so because it creates for the baby an external envelope of messages and adapts itself to fulfill the baby's needs. The above version exemplifies the connection between the skin and basic issues related to the establishment of the self. Only the concrete entrance into her sisters' skins provides her with the possibility of feeling a direct closeness to significant others. We should remember that this girl revenged herself on the witch because the witch killed and skinned her sisters. Even though the witch gave her treats, she still avenged her sisters and murdered the witch. This further clarifies that her entrance into her sisters' skins is an act of identification.

Bick (1968) related to the primary role of the baby's skin as connecting the various parts of the personality, which have not yet gone through differentiation. At the most primitive level, the parts of the personality are experienced as not being able to contain themselves. Hence, they need to be held together in a way that is experienced as passive—by the skin, which serves as a sort of container or border.

This conceptualization provides a perspective from which to understand the heroine's behaviour. Lacking a primary, containing maternal figure, the heroine enters her sisters' skins. She does so on the concrete level, thereby attaining warmth and protection, as well as on the abstract level: She "enters their skin" as a realization of the symbolic idiom that relates to the act of identification. Bick mentions that this role of holding together the parts of the self is associated with the internalization of an external object, which is experienced as being able to provide this function. Later, identification with this function of the object gives birth to the fantasy of internal and external realms, as indeed happens in the story, after the girl was raised by a good woman and no longer needed her sisters' skins. This process expresses the gradual coming into being of the psychic envelope that, at first, appears as a concrete skin, and later loosens, slowly becoming a place in which one can live. According to Bick, only after the containing function has been internalized can the concept of "realm" appear inside the self. The skins that cover the girl might express what Bick calls the "second-skin". This term relates to the "skin" through which dependence on the object is replaced by pseudo-independence through the improper use of certain mental functions, in order to create a substitute for the containing function of the skin.

Back to Donkey Skin

As mentioned at the beginning of this chapter, in Charles Perrault's verse tale, *Donkey Skin*, a maiden escapes her father's incestuous wishes by wearing the skin of a donkey. Entering the animal's skin in this tale has a special meaning related to the psychological transformation that a girl goes through when she encounters her father's lustful wishes. Different scholars have provided different interpretations to this fairy tale, varying from viewing the father's wish to marry his own daughter as a projection of the girl's oedipal desire (Bettelheim, 1976; Dundes, 1978; El-Shamy, 1999) to focusing on the active characteristics of the heroine, who succeeds in escaping from her lecherous father and takes charge of her life (Goldberg, 1997; Muhawi, 2001; Perco, 1993). Discussing the functions of the skin associated with the sense of identity, we choose to focus on the potential meanings of the realization of the idiom "living in her skin" as appearing in the tale. Whereas in the tale about the seven sisters, entering the heroine's sisters' skins might be understood as an act of identification, we suggest that entering an animal skin might attain different meanings, associated with issues related to a significant harm to the self, such as happens in sexual abuse. People who "feel good in their own skin" do not have to escape it. However, people suffering early and basic developmental disturbances do not feel good in their own skin. Whereas the tale about the seven sisters provides an image of a girl who suffers deep deficiency entering her sisters' skins, the tale *Donkey Skin* provides an image of psychological processes characterizing a girl escaping her own skin. First, it reveals the gloomy fact that girls falling prey to incest have no one to turn to for protection. Usually, the mother is passive and the family is silent or, worse, blames the victim. The new skin serves as some protection in the case of failed dependence, where authority and parental figures who are expected to protect their daughters fail to do so and betray their trust. The incest survivor can only escape from home if she wants to save her body and soul.

Understanding the function of the skin-ego in establishing identity, brings to the fore the image of "entering a donkey's skin" as expressing an identity transformation, or identity injury. Indeed, women who were sexually abused in their childhood rarely escape psychological problems, and many of them suffer from various disorders ranging from PTSD to borderline personality disorder (Herman, 1992). The donkey's skin serves to obliterate any feminine, or even human, identity, a theme common in women who survived incest and struggle for the rest of their lives in hiding any feminine features in an effort not to be too attractive, blaming themselves for their father's desire.

Milo and Raufman (2014) compared several oral versions of the tale about donkey skin (and, more specifically, a unique sub-type of this fairy tale in which the heroine is hiding not in a donkey's skin but, rather, in a wooden body) with blogs appearing on a website of sexually abused victims, pointing out the common themes that both kinds of narrative share. Their findings challenge the idea that views the heroine of the fairy tale as an active one who takes charge of her life. Instead, they suggest that the power of the narrative does not emerge from the figure of the heroine but is, rather, fueled by the narrators, who use their stories to voice and externalize female distress and oppression in a patriarchal society. Indeed, the donkey's skin story can be interpreted in both ways. We can focus on the princess finding a creative way to escape her father's oppression, or we can interpret the underlying problematic transformation of a young woman donning a donkey skin, entering a dystonic identity, dissociated from her own identity, perhaps reflecting the psychological mechanism of dissociation that is so common in incest cases. The Israeli versions of "wooden body" described in Milo and Raufman's study provide even a harsher expression of this idea. The wooden body enables objectifying the girl, who is no longer a human being but, rather, a wooden body, as presented in the tales. It also reflects the detachment of the girl from her sensorial body.

We cannot ignore the donkey's specific role in the plot. The striking contradiction between the heroine's beauty and the donkey's ugliness, mentioned in the introduction as part of Demy's film, draws our attention to the negative self-image that incest survivors easily develop. Blaming themselves (and being blamed by their environment) for what their lecherous father did, they feel dirty and ugly, more like a donkey than a beautiful princess.

It is possible to see how the functions of the skin in the above tales demonstrate the double meaning of the skin and the term skin-ego as formulated by Anzieu. The fairy tales illustrate the concrete function of the skin as holding and containing, and its direct involvement in the establishment of identity, as well as the symptoms that appear if these functions are lacking. The familiar drama described in the tales shows the multiple layers of the fairy tale's language, which brings together the concrete and the abstract, exposing the deep meaning of the idiom "living in their skin". From this perspective, entering the skin, as an act of identification, is not only an empathic act that enables adopting the point of view of the other. Instead, this is also an essential act, carried out in order to survive and establish a sense of identity by using a significant other. Whereas fairy tales reflect and echo social issues in a more cross-cultural narrative manner, many of the ideas presented above might be relevant to group therapy and could carry clinical implications.

The group skin-ego

Expanding his skin-ego concept, Anzieu developed the concept of the group skin-ego (1999), symbolically representing the group as an individual body. He argues that the image of the body and its schema are two of the group's principal organizers. Many scholars have related to the group as a whole psychic instances, such as group ego, group self, or group self-object (see Stone, 2005). This group ego is enveloped by an imaginary skin. Anzieu claims that the group builds a psychic group skin, an extension of the group and the individual skin-ego, constituted by the double support of both the individual skin-ego and the social "body". The image of the body, its skin and its schema, can also be society's principal organizers. Society builds a psychic social skin to imaginarily protect its existence and delimit its boundaries. Kaës and colleagues (2013) postulated that the psyche has a dual support: in the biological body and in the social body.

Following the three realms of Lacan, Anzieu identifies the real psychic group skin, delimiting group territory (occupied spaces, places, time for the group, the rhythm of the meetings, perhaps relevant to the holding function (Rutan et al., 2014) or the dynamic administration (Foulkes, 1975) of the group therapist), the imaginary group psychic skin, corresponding to fantasies and illusions about the group envelope, to organic metaphors in a language relative to the group (relevant to our discussion of somatic expressions), and the experience of continuity with the skin, and the symbolic group psychic skin, which includes signs and rituals pertaining to a sense of group belongingness (Yalom's cohesion).

Among the many functions of the group skin-ego, in the context of the functions Anzieu identifies for the individual skin-ego, are maintenance, containment, transparency, rigidity, signification, consensus, individuation, energizing, sexualisation, and more.[13] Many of these functions can be enhanced and facilitated by the group therapist (e.g., maintenance and containment are functions of the group therapist, see Rutan et al., 2014; Yalom & Leszsz, 2005).

In therapy groups, various phenomena can be perceived as testifying to the existence of group skin-ego. Resonance, a central concept in group analysis, occurs within the group and, although it is apparently not physical, it affects participants on the physical level. However, resonance is evident in the group in a way that testifies to the connections between external and internal events related to the group and its participants, serving as a kind of shared skin. Foulkes (1975) borrowed the term resonance from physics/music to designate the ability of group members to share each other's thoughts and emotions on a preverbal basis. In a way, this may be compared to the idea of a shared skin. The phenomenon of resonance is the individual's ability to slip into someone else's skin. As Pines (2003) noted, "Foulkes described resonance as the individual responses that group members make to shared events, each responding at their own level of attunement to the predominant affect in the group" (p. 512).

A group therapy vignette

A very anxious woman participated in a therapy group led by one of the authors. She was very withdrawn and did not talk at all during the first meetings. However, she slowly opened up, revealing a history of physical abuse by her father and emotional abuse by her mother. As a result, this woman became very self-critical and was sure that everything she did was wrong. She was very anxious in the group, constantly fearing that she was saying wrong things, burdening or hurting others. She had anxiety attacks outside the group that prevented her from leaving her house, but she made huge efforts not to miss even one group session. She felt that her body was exposed and unprotected from the world's pressures and that her skin could not prevent other people from intruding into her inner life. She described how, when she is very anxious, lying on her stomach helped her feel less anxious and more protected, as if in this position she manages better to cover and protect the more vulnerable parts of her body. In addition, whenever she felt the tension in her body heightening, she felt the need to cut herself, "to relieve the tension" (but without meaning to kill herself).

At one point, after a conflict she had experienced with her mother, she became suicidal and the group therapist was concerned that the group triggered too much anxiety that worsened her situation. He wondered (and brought it up in the group for discussion) whether the group was really good for her, since it evoked such strong emotions. Surprisingly, she started crying and begged the group therapist not to dismiss her from the group, since this was the first time she had ever felt a sense of belonging. She reported that the more she participated in the group—although her anxiety sometimes increased—the more protected she felt, as if a new envelope had formed around her. Lately, she said, her need to cut herself had decreased. The issue was elaborated in the group. The members were very supportive and caring. They were all involved in the dilemma of who should be included and excluded, and guaranteed the protective group skin. Eventually, after a thorough group discussion, she stayed in the group and continued her progress.

This vignette shows how the group skin can become a protective agent for some group members, to the extent of even partly compensating for a weak personal skin-ego. The fact that the woman's need to cut her skin decreased while her sense of belonging to the group increased is quite significant. It seems as if this patient was bound up with a skin-ego which failed to fulfill adequately its protective shield function: the sensations, emotions, and drives she would like to keep hidden inside were in constant danger of passing through the skin's cracks, becoming visible to others (Anzieu, 1989, p. 133). Lying on her belly could be a way to hide her inner parts. Cases of patients who cut themselves were addressed by Anzieu in discussing the containing function of the skin-ego.

The skin-ego as a mental representation emerges from the interplay between the mother's body and the child's, as well as from the responses the mother makes to the baby's sensations and emotions. At that stage, the skin-ego is imaginarily represented as an outer shell. The skin-ego cannot function as a container unless it has drives to contain, to localize in bodily sources, and, later, to differentiate. The drive is experienced only as an urge, as if its source is projected into areas of the body that are particularly open to stimulation. The failure of this containing function of the skin-ego results in two forms of anxiety: An instinctual excitation that is diffuse, constant, scattered, non-localizable, non-identifiable, unquenchable, results when the psychical topography consists of a kernel without a shell, the individual seeks a substitute shell in physical pain or psychical anxiety (which seems to be the case in the group vignette). In the second case, the envelope exists, but its continuity is broken into by holes. This skin-ego is a colander: thoughts and memories are only retained with difficulty.

Other group examples, involving resonance, could be seen on a more somatic level when, for example, one participant exposes herself by sharing a "revealing" and moving secret, and another group member starts shivering in response. Resonance lies at the basis of a member's identification with the other. As Brown (1994) stressed, "It is necessary for empathy, intuition, and the experience of being part of something that includes oneself, whether a dyad, a group, a species, or the cosmos" (p. 82). The processes which occur within the group echo within oneself, reverberating, leaving individuals with a deep sense of similarity among members. When no resonance occurs in a group, there is an inability to take part in a communicative exchange and dialogue. Yalom views resonance as the process behind universality (Yalom, 1995), which connects people at a deep, unconscious level, tuning in group members to the similarities that exist among them.

Based on findings emerging from our fairy tale research, it is possible to view some of the group's somatic experiences as hiding idiomatic expressions that could be relevant for understanding the group's dynamic. Here is one example from a group: A participant tells something horrifying to the group. The other participants find it difficult to relate to the horrifying content and remain silent. However, one of them has a somatic response: her skin reacts and the hair on the back of her neck rises. Another example is: One participant says something embarrassing, and another participant blushes in response. On the verbal level, nothing has been said. However, deciphering the idiomatic expression hidden behind the somatic reaction helps understand how one group member has just "put herself into the other one's skin".

From skin-ego through group-skin to the social unconscious

The role that the skin plays in establishing a sense of identity is highly related to social issues. According to Cavanagh and colleagues (2013, p. 2), "skin becomes a site for the projection and exposure of deep-seated cultural, political and psychical investments." The colour of the skin invites racial associations and projections. Skin is imbued with conscious and unconscious meanings, including all the social constructs that are also represented in the social unconscious, such as sex, gender, age, race, religion, nationality, and class. We can see how the skin contains both deep individual and social meanings.

Individual experiences of skin are also located within particular cultural and social contexts. A cultural studies' approach to skin, rooted in social, historical, and cultural contexts, offers critical analyses of the politics of skin, especially those tied to processes of racialization and other constructions of social difference.

The psyche of the individual depends on both the biological body and the social body. This is a bi-directional assumption that we share with Anzieu: a person's organic and social life both need the constant support of the person's psyche, and *vice versa*: this psyche constantly needs the living body and the social group for its continued existence. From the beginning, the ego is a body/skin-ego as well as a society ego.

Resonance is strongly related to the introjections and internalization of cultural codes by the infant. The early state of indistinction and fusion with the other encourages the incorporation of cultural coded models and binds the individual with the group to which s/he belongs. As Le Roy (1994) puts it: "This cultural basis continues to function during our whole life, it forms the frame of the feeling of 'us', as a part of our self, and of the phenomenon Foulkes called 'resonance'" (p. 183).

As mentioned in the introduction, the organism metaphor, comparing society to a body, is specifically used for the denigration of marginalized groups in a certain society, wherein the target group is portrayed as a threat to the integrity of the social body. Such an image, crystallizing stereotypes of those groups as inferior and dangerous, is extremely powerful, as it is addressing the primary somatic level of the social unconscious of the people from that society. These metaphors, from describing Jews as foreign intruders (or cancer) in the national body, to portraying the Japanese as a source of national indigestion, were used in the American anti-immigration movement of the early 1900s, the German anti-Semitic and Nazi movement and the anti-Japanese movement in the USA (1905–1945).

As pointed out above, skin is associated with conscious and unconscious meanings, including all the social aspects that reside in the social unconscious, which, according to Hopper and Weinberg (2011), includes aspects of family structure, class, and status group formations, ethnicity and classical classifications, gender and social roles, and age grades, as well as the basic beliefs and mores of a society.

Extrapolating from the small group to the large group (Schneider & Weinberg, 2003), we can assume that the large group identity (Volkan, 2001) serves as a large group skin-ego for communities, nations, and societies. Nations and countries are experienced in corporeal terms, so they seek to secure their borders (national skin-ego) from infiltration and penetration. In times of social stress and trauma, it serves well to protect its participants. Citizens need to feel that their country's borders have a containing–protective feature, especially when an outside enemy (real or imagined) threatens. Experiencing one's nation with insecure or porous boundaries is equivalent to the fear that one's skin will be penetrated (remember that the boundaries of one's ego expand to contain the entire space of one's nation within one's self). Thus, the image of the large group skin has a soothing and calming effect. However, mass media and politicians manipulate somatic images to describe a nation, knowing or sensing that people react to such an image on a primary level. The image of the body of a nation is used in the USA to describe the war over US borders, and the need to monitor internal intruders (Martin, 1990). In Israel, it is used to illustrate how national identity is inscribed in the Israeli body (Weiss, 2002). Especially nowadays, when immigrants flood European countries, whose borders are open, easily evoking primitive fears among citizens, it is easy to use those bodily and nation-skin images to advocate walled states. Popular politicians manipulate popular imagination enmeshing body and state, addressing fantasies of control and order, compelling punitive forms of governmental cleanliness and purifying violence. The image of a wall around a country, to prevent intruders, terrorists, smugglers, or immigrants, whether it is the Great Wall in ancient China, the Israeli West Bank barrier, or the USA–Mexico border fence, is especially appealing, not only due to its protective realistic function, but also as an image of a national skin-ego where state and body fantasies merge.

Anzieu preferred to let the term skin-ego remain ambiguous—at least enough to wonder whether it is concrete or metaphoric. He actually hinted that it is both. He was less ambiguous about the term "group skin", and clarified that it is a metaphor. We should also clarify that, just as the *image* of the body and its schema are the principal organizers of the group, meaning that the group ego is enveloped by an *imaginary* skin, we argue that, within the context of the social unconscious, is an *image* of the social skin. However, we claim that this social skin resides along the seam between the concrete and the symbolic, the somatic and the mental, and whose impact is strong enough to protect the members of that society and enhance their social identity.

What makes the members of a specific social grouping feel that they have something in common and that they belong to the same community? It is especially puzzling when we talk about large groups (Schneider & Weinberg, 2003), where boundaries are loose. The somatic dimension of the social unconscious, and the image of the social skin which is part of it, can explain it to some extent. Resonance mechanisms, helping people to "enter one another's skin", make them feel that they have something in common, and encourage the social identity and sense of belonging to the large social group.

CHAPTER FOUR

Eyes and envy: reading Grimms' *One-eye, Two-eyes and Three-eyes* and its Jewish parallels

> "Oh, beware, my lord, of jealousy! It is the green-eyed monster which doth mock the meat it feeds on"
>
> (Shakespeare, 1988: *Othello*, Act III, Scene III)

Envy and fear of being envied is ubiquitous. Patients in therapy groups who talk about their fear of inciting envy are not rare. In one of our groups, a participant described the conflict she faces when she wants to show her virtues and be proud of them, but at the same time she feels the eyes of the other group members piercing her like knives. In response, another participant resonated, describing how, at the family table, when he was talking about his experiences at work, his father was sitting silently, just staring at him with piercing eyes. He felt that his father was dissatisfied with what he had said, silently scolding him, as if stabbing him with his gaze. The experience of the other's eyes as a knife is penetrating and powerful. We, the authors, have our own childhood memories. One of us remembers a dark night in which she walked alone in the darkness, sensing the eyes of a threatening stranger as if stabbing her back, pushing her legs to walk faster, running away from the threat. The penetrating eyes of the other, creating a physical sensation, is not just an individual, private, one-time experience, but, rather, resonates with the experience of many people.

In the case of Cacilie, appearing in Freud's *Studies on Hysteria* (1895d), the patient traced the neural pain she felt in her face back to an adolescence memory where she was resting in bed under the strict supervision of her rigid grandmother. The sharp pain she felt between her eyes was explained, in her analysis, as being associated with her grandmother's penetrating stare and the thought that her grandmother suspected her of something. In this case, the unpleasant feeling of being under the scrutinizing eye of someone is converted into somatic pain. In addition to the idiomatic expression "a piercing/penetrating stare", converted in Cacilie's case into a somatic symptom, it looks as if another idiomatic expression is embedded here. This expression has many facets and modalities in folklore and popular beliefs, usually called "The evil eye", and seems to play a role in the foundation matrices of many peoples.

The fear of the evil eye is manifested in many rituals and customs, as well as many genres in the popular folk literature. Amulets, charms, and decorations with eye-like symbols, aimed to protect against and repel the evil eye, are common across countries such as Turkey, Greece, Albania, Egypt, Iran, Israel, Southern Italy, Asian tribes and cultures, as well as other regions around the world. In Arabic, it is called *ayn al-ḥasūd* (eye of the envious). The evil eye is also mentioned in the Bible (Proverbs 23:6: "Eat thou not the bread of him that hath an evil eye, neither desire thou his dainty meats"). This is only part of the rich tradition with its various expressions of a well-known phenomenon around the world.

The case presented in this chapter exemplifies how fairy tales might personify the evil eye, embodied as a jealous sister, a common motif prevalent in the folk tradition of various peoples. We chose to focus on the famous version of the Grimm brothers *One-eye, Two-eyes and Three-eyes* [ATU 511] as well as the Jewish–Bulgarian and Jewish–Libyan tales "Tulips/Jasmine for the eyes" [IFA 16243 and 6710]). In accordance with the central idea of this book, we examine the way in which these fairy tales, which are part of the foundation matrices of the people who tell them, express in words somatic, sensorial experiences related to envy and avarice. Exposing realizations of idiomatic expressions related to eyes in these tales helps to touch upon the thought processes and modes of expression operating in the tales, viewing the plot in a new light, as well as exploring different aspects of the social unconscious.

As in previous chapters, two theoretical models are involved in this methodological process: the first relates to the conceptualization of the primary levels of mental organization, governed by the world of somatic sensations and senses, including the sense of seeing. The second model relates to the identification of a psycho-linguistic phenomenon characterizing fairy tales: the realization of idiomatic expression, which points to the location of the genre on the borderline between verbal and pictorial thinking. Identifying idioms such as *"an eye for an eye"*, *"to keep an eye"*, *"to turn a blind eye"*, and other idioms appearing also in the German language from which the Grimms' tale is taken, helps to offer an interpretation which was unavailable otherwise. Decoding these expressions leads to a better understanding of the "social mind" of the society in which these tales are told and preserved.

Two Jewish tales, also with an emphasis on the eye, recorded in the Israeli Folktale Archive (IFA) and presenting similar themes, are discussed in the same context. The comparative discussion enables us to learn about cross-cultural primary elements operating in those tales, such as the development of envy as a basic concept of the mind and its function in the fairy tale, as well as unconscious processes in a specific society and societal context.

One-eye, Two-eyes and Three-eyes

A woman had three daughters: The eldest had one eye in the middle of her forehead, the second had two eyes like ordinary people, the third had two eyes on the side of her head and a third in the middle of her forehead. Her mother and sisters scorned Little Two-Eyes because she was like other people and treated her badly, leaving her only their leftovers to eat.

One day Little Two-Eyes was sent to the field to tend to the goat, she sat down and cried as she had been given so little to eat and when she looked up a woman was standing beside her. The woman asked her why she was crying. Little Two-Eyes explained and the wise woman told her to say to the goat

> Little goat, bleat
> lay me a table
> with lots to eat

A beautifully spread table would stand before her, and Little Two-eyes could eat as much as she wanted. The woman then told Little Two-eyes that when she had had enough to eat she simply had to say

> Little goat, bleat
> Take the table away
> I've had all I can eat

and the table would vanish. The wise woman then left and Little Two-eyes spoke the words the woman had told her would summon the table, and, to her surprise, there it stood. Little Two-eyes ate until she was full and said the words the woman told her would make the table disappear, and immediately it was all gone. Little Two-eyes returned home in the evening and found the plate of leftovers her sisters had left for her, but she did not touch it.

The next day she went out again with the goat and left the scraps given to her; after a time, her sisters began to notice this and told their mother. So Little One-eye was sent to go with Little Two-eyes when she drove the goat to pasture to see if someone was giving her food and drink. Little Two-eyes suspected this was the reason Little One-eye was accompanying her and sang Little One-eye a song to make her one eye fall asleep. Little Two-eyes then summoned the table and ate as before. On returning home, Little One-eye told her mother that the fresh air made her so tired she fell asleep and that was why she did not see what Little Two-eyes had done, so the next day the mother sent Little Three-eyes to watch Little Two-eyes when she went out with the goat. Little Two-eyes suspected that Little Three-eyes had been sent to watch her and so meant to sing her song to make her three eyes fall asleep but instead she sang a song to only make two of her eyes fall asleep. Little Three-eyes shut her third eye though it was still awake, so when Little Two-eyes thought her sister was fast asleep she said the rhyme and ate and drank from the little table, though all the while Little Three-eyes blinked her eye and watched. When they returned home, Little Three-eyes told her mother what she had seen. Her mother then, in rage that Little Two-eyes thought to live better than her family, fetched a knife and killed the goat.

Little Two-eyes sat in the meadow and cried having seen what her mother had done. Just as before when she looked up the wise woman stood beside her and asked why she wept. Little Two-eyes explained and the wise woman told her to bury the heart of the goat as it would bring her luck. That evening Little Two-eyes buried the heart before the door just as the wise woman had told her and the next morning there, where she had buried the heart, stood a beautiful tree which had leaves of silver and fruit of gold growing on it.

The mother told Little One-eye to climb the tree and break off some fruit, but as Little One-eye tried to take hold of one of the golden apples, the bough sprang out of her hands. This happened every time she reached for it. The mother then told Little Three-eyes to climb the tree and break off some fruit since with her three eyes she could see much better than Little One-eye. Little Three-eyes was no more successful than her older sister, and at last the mother climbed up and tried in vain to break off a single piece of fruit. Little Two-eyes then volunteered to try. Her sisters told her that she would not succeed with her two eyes. To their great surprise, Little Two-eyes managed to pluck off a whole apron full of the golden fruit, and her mother took them from her. But instead of treating Little Two-eyes better, her sisters and mother were jealous that only she could pick the golden fruit and were even more unkind than before.

One day, a Knight came riding along. Little One-eye and Little Three-eyes pushed Little Two-eyes under an empty cask nearby so the Knight would not see her. The Knight stopped to admire the beautiful tree and asked whom it belonged to, saying that whoever would give him a twig from the tree could have whatever they wanted. The two sisters told him that the tree belonged to them and that they would certainly break a twig off for him. But just as before, the twigs and fruit bent away from their hands whenever they got close. The Knight exclaimed that it was odd that the owners of the tree could not break anything from it, yet the sisters insisted the tree was theirs. Little Two-eyes, who was still hidden under the empty cask, rolled a couple of golden apples to the Knight's feet. When the Knight asked where the apples had come from, the two sisters confessed they had another sister but she had been hidden away because she had two eyes like normal people. The Knight demanded to see Little Two-eyes, who came happily from under the cask and told the Knight that the tree was indeed hers. So Little Two-eyes climbed up the tree and broke off a small branch with its silver leaves and golden fruit with ease and gave it to the Knight. The Knight proceeded to ask Little Two-eyes what she would like, as she was entitled to whatever she wanted. Little Two-eyes asked to be taken away from the suffering she had at the hands of her mother and sisters. So the Knight lifted

Little Two-eyes on to his horse and took her to live at his father's castle. There he treated her to beautiful clothes and food and drink. They fell in love and he married her.

The two sisters believed that they were lucky to have kept the beautiful tree as Little Two-eyes and the Knight first set off for the castle, but, to their dismay, the very next morning they awoke to find that the tree had vanished. When Little Two-eyes woke and looked out of her window, she saw, with delight, that the tree had grown outside the castle.

When two poor women came to the castle to beg one day, Little Two-eyes looked at them and realized that they were her sisters. Little Two-eyes took them in and made them welcome. The sisters then repented of ever having been so mean to their sister.

The main issue in this tale is quite clear and deals with envy and covetousness: the mother and the two irregular daughters envy Two-eyes because she was ordinary. Whereas envy and covetousness are pretty common in fairy tales, on the overt level, its appearing in our tale under discussion is, apparently, bizarre. In addition, the tale may be considered unusual since it is not the youngest who is different from the other two (as is common in fairy tales), but, rather, the middle sister. However, what is salient here is the affinity between envy and eyes.

Usually, the verb "to see" is connected, in common language, to the verb "to understand". When we say, "I see what you're saying", we mean, "I understand what you're saying." This is true for many languages. In Genesis, when Adam and Eve ate from the tree of knowledge, "their eyes were opened, and they knew" (Genesis 3:7). The sense of knowledge is directly connected to seeing. In another chapter. we demonstrate how concrete blindness in a tale might be the fairy tale's way to describe a psychological inability to see things, meaning: to understand. A king who could not understand his daughter's feelings, all of a sudden, and with no special explanation, suffers physical blindness. The ability to see is connected to the most basic and central abilities required in order to function adequately in everyday life. In our discussed tale, an irregular situation (of the eyes) evokes uncontrolled envy. However, unlike the king who became physically as well as metaphorically blind, in this tale there are some other idiomatic expressions hidden behind the concrete plot. We are dealing with idioms such as "to turn a blind eye" (also exits in German: *Ein Auge zudrücken*, to close one eye), "to watch" (*Ein Auge werfen*: to keep an eye), and to have "eyes in one's head" (*Sie hat Augen im Kopf*). After discussing these idioms and their functioning in the Grimms' tale, we discuss some other idioms, such as "an eye for an eye", which attain a concrete form in two Jewish parallels of the Grimms' tale.

Decoding the idiom Sie hat Augen im Kopf (she has eyes in her head)

The middle daughter deals with reality better than her sisters. Not only does she gain the prince, as well as the fairy's magical help, she is the only one who looks normal and ordinary, therefore she fits into society and normal life. It might be said that she is blessed. What is her blessing? After all, unlike Cinderella or other heroines who struggle with the same situation of envious sisters, we are not told that she is more beautiful (at least not directly). What makes her blessed is the fact that her eyes are normal, and may function normally. The metaphorical meaning of the German idiom: *Sie hat Augen im Kopf* (she has eyes in her head) may be perceived as a precise translation of her existential situation, which enables her to face reality effectively. Furthermore, the sisters' envy is also described through the eyes: many expressions related to envy use the word "eye" in order to express mental ideas. For example, "to poke out someone's eyes" means to make someone jealous. The eyes also serve, in the tale, as a way of dealing with reality and to watch for harm and dangers. When we say about someone that s/he "turns a blind eye", we mean that s/he prefers to ignore something that s/he does not want to deal with. This expression also exists in German, as it is common to say: *ein Auge zudrücken* (to close your eyes, meaning to ignore, not to pay attention). Indeed, when Two-eyes wishes to escape from One-eye's observing gaze, she makes her turn a blind eye. When One-eye actually closes her one eye, she cannot function in a useful way. Another expression existing in German, describing an opposite situation, refers to the need to keep your eyes open in order to cope with reality: *Die Augen offen halten* (keep your eyes open: to watch, to pay attention).

In his book *Crowds and Power* (1973), Canetti states that the most frightening thing for human beings is the unknown:

> There is nothing that man fears more than the touch of the unknown. He wants to see what is reaching toward him, and to be able to recognize or at least classify it. Man always tends to avoid physical contact with anything strange. (p. 15)

In the Grimms' tale, One-eye and Three-eyes represent the bizarre, the strange, and the unknown. Their distortion is a salient feature in the tale that moves the plot forward. Their envy is explained only as a response to Two-eyes' ordinary look. It is inevitable for the readers/listeners not to feel aversion, disgust, and revulsion towards these distorted, unusual characters. The strangeness in this case is presented as dangerous for ordinarily functioning human beings. It threatens to devastate and destroy their wellbeing.

This idea is strongly connected to Freud's "The 'uncanny'" (*Das Unheimliche*, 1919h), describing a sense of estrangement within the home, the presence of something threatening and unknown that lies within the bounds of the intimate. One-eye and Three-eyes are the strangers that live at home; the strangers who are "inside us". They are not the monsters living in the dark forest, neither are they the witches hiding beyond the far mountains. Instead, they are the heroine's own sisters, her own flesh and blood. Their irregular eyes mark their uncanniness.

It is worth noting that the eye is associated with the uncanny in another literary masterpiece: *The Sandman*, written by Hoffman in 1817, published five years after the first volume of the Grimms' collection. Hoffman was one of the most influential authors in German Romanticism of the early nineteenth century. Later, we elaborate how Romantic ideas are manifested in the Grimms' tale, reflecting the changing cultural needs of the society at their time, during the transition from feudalism to early capitalism. Discussing the uncanny in Hoffman's story, Freud suggests that social taboos reveal the common assumption that what is hidden from public eye must be a dangerous threat. We interpret the expression "what is hidden from the public eye" as a possible counterpart for what we now call "the social unconscious". Freud draws on the idea of being robbed of one's eyes as the most striking instance of uncanniness in Hoffman's tale:

> A study of dreams, phantasies and myths has taught us that anxiety about one's eyes, the fear of going blind, is often enough a substitute

for the dread of being castrated. The self-blinding of the mythical criminal, Oedipus, was simply a mitigated form of the punishment of castration. (Freud, 1919h, p. 230)

Canetti (1973) points out that "one of the most striking traits of the inner life of a crowd is the feeling of being persecuted" (p. 12). In our discussed tale, Two-eyes represents this idea, while being persecuted by her mother and sisters, who might represent the uncanny: on the one hand they are her own flesh and blood, sharing the same home and even the same genes, and, on the other hand, so different, strange, unknown, dreadful, and dangerous. When Canetti discusses the fear of the bizarre, strange, and unknown, he relates to the need to *see*. Although he views this fear as universal, it is possible that in the times when the Grimms published their collection in the Germany of the nineteenth century, this fear attained a unique form. In order to address this issue, we first discuss some aspects related to the Grimms' collection.

The brothers Grimm collection

A large body of material has been dedicated to the question of the authenticity of the Grimms' collection, and whether these tales reflect "the German spirit" (see, for example, Dégh, 1979; Dundes, 1987b; Harshbarger, 2013; Ihms, 1975; Kohn, 1950; Zipes, 1977; and others). Ihms (1975) claims that nationalism motivated the brothers, who believed that these folk tales expressed the spirit of the nation. He also argues that some of the tales reflect the political situation of their time. For example, Red Riding Hood symbolizes the freedom-seeking Jacobeans, who wore a red hood. The wolf in this tale represents Napoleon and the French, etc. However, other scholars provided different perspectives to understand this plot, which may be found not only in the Grimms' collection but in many other cultures and eras. It is evident, for example, that the Grimms were well aware of the French version published by Charles Perrault more than 100 years earlier and were influenced by it, as well as by other collections and mythologies.[14] Dundes, among others, warns against the common tendency of basing psychoanalytical interpretations solely on the Grimms' collection. He reminds us, that since psychoanalysis began in the German speaking world ... it was inevitable that Freud and other early psychoanalysts interested in the content of folktales would turn to the major, principle corpus of tales in German, namely the celebrated *Kinder- und Hausmärchen* of the brothers Grimm. (Dundes, 1987b, p. 50)

This tendency is problematic for many reasons, mostly because of the editing and censorship made by the brothers Grimm. In a paper dedicated to symbols in dreams and folklore, Freud and Oppenheim (1958[1911]) were sensitive enough not to rely on the Grimms' collection, but, rather, on traditional German tales contained in the pages of *Anthropophyteia* (1904–1913), a journal founded by folklorist F. S. Krauss in Vienna. However, many psychoanalysts still tend to base their interpretation on the Grimms' collection. Dundes points out that "the collection cannot be regarded as totally representative of German folktales at the beginning of the nineteenth century" (1987b, p. 52). Dundes further claims that "despite the fact that the Grimms ... called for the scientific collection of authentic folktales as they were orally told by peasants, the evidence reveals that the Grimm brothers failed to practice what they preached" (p. 52). Following this, as well as many other contributions demonstrating how the Grimms' collection is not representative of the German folk spirit, we should be careful not to analyze and interpret the above version as necessarily reflecting that. However, the Grimms' version can be viewed and analyzed in the light of the socio-cultural-political context of German Romanticism. While discussing the revolutionary rise of the Romantic fairy tale in Germany, Zipes (1977) points out that "the socio-cultural basis of the (Romantic) fairy tale is intricately linked to that of the folk tale" (p. 412), and that

> ... the folk tale itself was revolutionized to enable the Romantic to depict the ambulant nature of the rise of enlightened ideas, rationalism and free enterprise. This undertaking was both conscious and unconscious and represented one of the major accomplishments of the Romantics.... the fairy tale may have timeless or universal qualities like the folk tale, but its historical origin informs or even limits in a positive way its universal appeal ... valid generalization can still be made despite their singular qualities. (p. 429)

Comparing this version to other versions presenting similar motifs (such as the Jewish versions) helps us to draw conclusions that go beyond one single case. Two points are important here: first, there is a complete resemblance between the main theme of the plot discussed here, and the meanings of the idiomatic expressions hidden behind it, as they exist in the German language. The second point relates to the fact that, although this particular version does not necessarily reflect the German folk spirit, the German social and cultural climate of their time easily embraced many motifs of this tale, whose popularity is unquestionable. As Harshbarger (2013) points out, German-speaking children were exposed to several printed and successively revised versions of the story collected by the brothers Grimm during the years 1812 and 1857, an era during which, according to Greenfeld, German "nationalism was speedily becoming the framework of the deepest individual and collective identity" (quoted in Harshbarger, p. 495). Apparently, in addition to being embraced by the Germans, some argue that the Grimms' collection can be viewed as part of the German collective identity, as an effort to create this national identity, even if it was not "originally" German.[15]

According to Dégh (1979), the Grimms' collection contributed to structuring German nationalism. She questions its folkloric nature, suggesting that these tales were created from scraps of accidentally found traditional materials. However, as a whole, they encouraged an ideology for German nationalism and folk romanticism. Hopper and Weinberg (2011) claim that collective memories structure the social unconscious, which is the glue of the sense of belonging to a certain society. The Grimms' tales might have served to strengthen the feeling of belonging by creating a shared past. As Durkheim (1971) puts it,

> collective representations remind the group of its ideals, thus not only reinforcing the ideals in question, but also promoting the mutual recognition of the reality and potency of the ideas involved, thereby promoting the solidarity of the group. . . . they give rise to euphoria and collective strength . . . . (p. 229)

Apparently, the Grimms' collection gained popularity in Nazi Germany. Ideologists of the Third Reich viewed the tales' heroes as models for the desirable "fundamental Aryan German" prototype and as pioneers of racism. The Nazis demanded that every German household own a copy of the Grimms' collection. Their ideological arguments were that the tales stimulated the fighting spirit and the will for victory among Germans and increased German self-consciousness.

After the Second World War, the Grimm brothers' tales were accused of encouraging German cruelty and even facilitating the atrocities of the war and the Holocaust, and the books were removed from the shelves for a while. As Dégh pointed out,

> The opinion spread that German tales, particularly those of the Grimms, were responsible for Auschwitz, Buchenwald, the horrors of the war, and extreme racial intolerance ... some critics ordered that the tales be eliminated from school textbooks and also that Grimm storybooks be withdrawn from circulation. (Dégh, 1979, p. 96)

However, Dégh reminds us that the authorities failed to consider that the collection of the brothers Grimm was "anything but pure German, even if the Nazis had claimed it was" and that "the brothers and their collaborators didn't hesitate to Germanize good stories from foreign sources" (Dégh, 1979, p. 96).[16]

In fact, the Grimms' collection is no crueller than many other fairy tale collections of other cultures. Dégh was not the only one to remind us that "the tales of any people could be considered gruesome and that the Grimm versions are not among the worst ... nations have always been interested in their roots and in past greatness" and that "like the Grimms in Germany, other scholars of the 19th century also saw the vestiges of their lost myths in folktales and legends" (Dégh, 1979, p. 97). This notion is important, because it testifies to both the component of cruelty in folktales in general, including the tale about One-eye, Two-eyes, and Three-eyes (and its possible functions in the human mind and in society), and the specific form it attains in each particular version and context.

In general, when discussing the affinity between fairy tales and society, we can talk about a bi-directional influence: Fairy tales reflect social issues and at the same time are part of the creation of norms, values, and social trends. This is, of course, true for the Grimms' collection and German society.

Unconscious and historical processes in German society

Every single version of a folk tale is a blend of both universal and local aspects. The Grimms' version of *One-eye, Two-eyes and Three-eyes*, first published in 1812, reflects and echoes in its way some universal anxieties alongside issues unique for this particular version written in the epoch of German Romanticism. Can we assume that German society at that time was preoccupied with these issues, whether consciously or unconsciously?

Zipes (1977) points out that "all the romantics sought to contain, comprehend and comment on the essence of the changing times in and through the fairy tale ..." (p. 410). "In its early phase the fairy tale reflects the lack of real possibilities for social participation desired by talented members who wanted to create something new and questioned all existing institutions" (p. 420). According to Zipes, the Romantics sought to open up society, longing for non-alienating conditions of existence, particularly through the awareness that human beings have free will to rationally determine their destinies.

The middle sister in the tale *One-eye, Two-eyes and Three-eyes*, with her two eyes in her head, extracts herself from the authoritarian rule of the mother, expressing longing for free will and emancipation. She might well represent the Romantics' struggle of the oppressed wishing to oppose forces which blocked self-development and self-government. As Rusch-Feja (1995) puts it,

> the maturation process is a process of individuation. The heroine extracts herself from a problematic situation, usually within the family context. In most cases, the events of the tale begin when the problematic situation becomes unbearable for the heroine, forcing her to action. Only rarely are the events stimulated by outside factors, by the age of the heroine, or by actions or desires of the parents. (p. 20)

The relevance of this notion to the situation of the Romantics in Germany is self-evident. Rusch-Feja further claims that

> ... she also attains new awareness, either with the help of others or as a result of her searching, wandering, or patient waiting. At the end of this period of waiting, wandering, or searching is usually a rebirth image ... and the emergence of a higher consciousness. (p. 20)

Associating the act of "seeing" with issues of self-awareness (or insight), as appearing in the tale about Two-eyes, helps in learning about the way in which the fairy tale provides an illustrative expression of a mental idea: By using the image of a two-eyed sister who differs from her other sisters whose ability to see things is injured (resulting in a lower degree of development), the fairy tale personifies an abstract idea. Rusch-Feja points out,

> In the process of individuation, symbiotic relationships are severed, the confrontation with evil or evil-intentioned, jealous persons leads to recognition and integration of one's shadow, and furthermore, the girl's ability to use her own ingenuity and powers lead to greater self-assertion and a balanced, more stable and richer personality. (p. 20)

In addition to the fact that Two-eyes might well represent issues of individuation, her in-between status in the family could represent the in-between status of the Romantics, who, according to Zipes, were caught between the critique of the philistine quality of their own middle-class and critique of the decadence of the nobility. They worked in a transitional period in which neither peasants nor workers constituted a united revolutionary force in Germany, a period of change in German society from feudalism to early capitalism (Zipes, 1977, p. 422).[17]

Whereas, in reality, the rebellions encounter the limitations of social institutions, which slowly integrate them into the system, the fairy tale could provide hope and aspiration for a better world. In this context, Zipes mentions that the anti-authoritarian and erotic symbols in the romantic fairy tale indicate that the Romantics were aware of the "betrayed" revolution in Germany.

The Grimms' collection and German foundation matrix

Although we cannot take the Grimms' collection as a pure folk creation, it is possible that some German foundation matrix characteristics are reflected in this tale. The question of whether Germans are inferior or superior to other nations exercised the German people for centuries. The words of the German popular song, "Deutschland, Deutschland über alles" (literally, "Germany, Germany above all"), expressing the preoccupation of German society with issues of superiority and inferiority, were chosen as the national anthem of Germany in 1922. One might not be surprised to find that these words were written in 1841, less than thirty years after the first Grimms' volume was published. The relationship among the sisters in the Grimms' version can be understood in terms of the struggle between inferior and superior forces.

During the sixteenth and seventeenth centuries, the German third estate became crippled and divided. The German middle-class sought ways to compromise with the nobility which would enable them to share in the government and safeguard their vested interests. These compromises led to bourgeoisie dependence on the state. Zipes (1977) describes the national character of the Germans as wretched and the characteristics of the German bourgeoisie as industriousness, duty, and morality. The study of the national character engaged many sociologists and anthropologists in the first half of the twentieth century, but declined in the second half, perhaps due to the impact of the Second World War and the traumatic burden that such explanations carried after National Socialism (Yair, 2017). Putting it simply, the national character is similar to the concept of the habitus presented by Elias (1996, see later) or to the foundation matrix postulated by Foulkes (1975).

The role played by the German bourgeoisie during the Romantic period led to the stabilization of a society in transition from late feudalism to early capitalism and reinforcement of aristocratic rules. Since folk tales inevitably dealt with power and how to order one's life within a realm that greatly resembled a medieval hierarchy, it was natural to the Romantics to reutilize this genre for their own purposes. Their distress was tied to the common wretchedness of the German people and they sought to strike a common chord to which the German people might respond.

In this context, it is worth noting Brewer, who reminds us that

> Even our deepest needs are seen by some modern scholars as "socially constructed" ... It may be that the latest forms of fairy tale will indeed fulfil the same social purpose as earlier fairy tales in teaching lessons, in meeting specific needs and urging socially acceptable solutions, but the personal needs and social constructs may be different. (2003, p. 27)

We should ask what kind of needs characterized the people in the Grimms' era.

The fairy tales (and other literature of that time) served the function of inventing an idealized past from whence entitlements can be derived. The nineteenth century knew this idealization of one's own country very well. The nation acquired a very high value for which a citizen was willing to die, because it was more important than the individual. We shall see later that these issues preoccupy other nations as well.

So far, we have discussed the fairy tale in the light of a socio-political context. We seek to explore the affinity between this socio-political-historical situation and the German foundation matrix. Norbert Elias, the German–British sociologist, had a profound influence on Foulkes' thinking and his conceptualization of group analysis. In his book, *The Germans* (1996), Elias connected social–historical events with the habitus of individuals belonging to a certain society. By "habitus" Elias means "second nature" or "embodied social learning" (Elias, 1994). This concept is strongly related to the social unconscious.

Elias argues that, starting around the twelfth century, long-term processes of state formation in Europe, where the power of central authority grew, contributed to the gradual monetarization and commercialization of social relations. In the case of Germany, there were deep-rooted obstacles to state centralization, and to the development of democratic values, attitudes, and institutions. He explains that the large territory occupied by the German-speaking people and the size of their population led them to encounter greater difficulties regarding unification and state centralization than the English and French people. This became deeply rooted in the habitus and traditions of a majority of Germans. Elias even goes further to claim that it led eventually to the rise of Nazism.

Germany (or actually The Holy Roman Empire of German Nation that preceded it) experienced a massive power loss[18] in the sixteenth century when, largely in conjunction with wars between Catholic and Protestant princes and dukes, the medieval empire broke up. From the sixteenth century to the end of the nineteenth century, the Germans (or their predecessors) were viewed as non-militaristic and weak, very different from the dominant outside image of the Germans throughout the twentieth century, which has been as a warlike people. As a result, according to Elias, the Germans became painfully aware of their low status in the rank hierarchy of European states and developed chronic doubts regarding their own self-worth.

We might wonder whether these social processes are reflected in the Grimms' fairy tale cited above.

National narcissism revisited

The Germans were not the only ones who were preoccupied with issues of superiority and inferiority during their history. In fact, questions of national pride and uniqueness of a specific society accompany many countries and nations. A certain level of narcissistic pride in one's country is healthy and even necessary for the unification of a nation, while its extreme expression (such as in the German Nazism or other nationalistic movements) is pathological and dangerous.

Jews used to consider themselves as "the chosen people". Weinberg (2009) identifies this idea as one of the assumptions embedded in the social unconscious of Jewish people in Israel, unconsciously affecting their behavior and attitude towards other nations. Apparently, it can lead either to an arrogant attitude based on a deep feeling of entitlement and superiority, but also to an over-responsible and moralistic attitude with excessive self-criticism.

In his book *Why the Japanese Are a Superior People*, De Mente (2009) argues that Japanese people believe that they are superior to other nations. He points out that Japanese even base their claim of superiority on neuroscientific evidence. He attributes the special knowledge and skills of the Japanese to the premise that they are primarily right-brain orientated as a result of their vowel-heavy language. He claims that the fact that the Japanese are able to use both sides of their brains gives them significant advantages over predominately left-brained people. As Weinberg (2007) identifies, myths are part of the social unconscious: The core of the traditional Japanese superiority complex probably derives from the myth that Japan was created by divine beings and that the Japanese were descendants of these same superior creatures. De Mente claims that Americans, Germans, English, and French in particular have traditionally been afflicted with a very conspicuous and destructive superiority complex that is a distinctive facet of their national characters. The Japanese also harbor a superiority complex that is as strong as, if not stronger than, that of most other nationalities (in this context it is interesting to note the alliance between Germany and Japan during the Second World War). The striving for superiority and overcoming enemies is well reflected in fairy tales of all peoples and societies, in which the hero overcomes the villain. Propp, in his *Morphology of the Folktale* (1968), describes the constant series of functions that every fairy tale follows. Whereas function sixteen refers to the struggle between the hero and the villain, function eighteen refers to the victory, in which the hero defeats the villain. Propp based his formulation on Russian fairy tales, but later scholars have shown its validity in the tales of other communities as well (Ben-Amos, 1967; Dundes, 1964).

Freud (1921c), in his *Group Psychology and the Analysis of the Ego*, has already mentioned that "every little canton looks down upon the others with contempt" (p. 131). There is a universal tendency of people to see their own groups as better than other groups, and a desire of nations to inflate themselves. Some term this universal phenomenon as "collective narcissism" (Bourdieu, 1996; Golec de Zavala et al., 2009) and warn that it leads to ethnocentrism, judging another culture solely by the values and standards of one's own culture. It also reminds us of Tajfel's (1982) famous experiments in social psychology about in-group and out-group bias: When someone is in a group to which we belong, we will have positive views of them and give them preferential treatment. Out-group people are viewed more negatively and given worse treatment.

Cross-cultural aspects

Whereas we focus on the Grimm version, it is worth noting that this tale-type is found in many other folk tale collections throughout the world, mainly in Europe but not only. In the Aarne–Thompson tale-types index classification (1961), this tale is classified as AT 511, found in countries such as Finland, Sweden, Estonia, Lithuania, Denmark, Scotland, France, Ireland, Austria, Hungary, Serbia, Croatia, Poland, Russia, Greece, as well as India, Franco-America, English-America and Spanish-America. This large distribution raises questions regarding its functions and meanings in human experience.

The above fairy tale resonates with a famous Greek myth about three old women who shared one eye, which in a way points to the opposite social processes embedded in society at large: The Graiai (or Graeae) were three ancient sea spirits who personified the white foam of the sea. They shared among themselves a single detachable eye and tooth. Perseus stole these and compelled the Graiai to reveal the hidden location of their sister, Gorgones. This myth can be interpreted in many ways. One possible hidden meaning can be about the illusion of separateness and individuality that is so common to modern Western culture. A person can rely on being a separate individual in possession of a skin with a clear boundary between inside and outside (see our discussion about the skin-ego in Chapter Three), between one's senses and the others' senses. However, the group analytic perspective, expressed eloquently by Dalal (1998), is that "there is no such a thing as an individual that exists apart from and outside the social" (p. 12). He followed Elias (1994), who claim that there is no such thing as a self-contained "monad" called the individual which stands in "glorious" opposition to society.

The shared eye of the three Graiai stands in contrast to the One-eye, Two-eyes, and Three-eyes heroines of the Grimms' tale, teaching us that deep inside we have something in common, and that we share more than we can imagine. Some argue that it is the social unconscious of people from specific societies that creates this illusion of separateness, and divides us into *us* and *them* (see Berman et al., 2000), an idea which is evident in the fairy tale genre, characterized with a complete dichotomy between the good hero, with which the community who tells this tale can identify, and the bad villain, to whom the community attributes all evilness in the world.

The common theme in the Graiai myth and the fairy tale about One-eye, Two-eyes, and Three-eyes, is that, in both, the eye is related to the existence of unnatural, as-if supernatural creatures, that do not exist in the real world (a girl with one or three eyes, or three women with one eye). Both stories revive and echo an archaic, ancient world governed by nominostic and demonic forces. However, the fairy tale includes also a human natural being (Two-eyes) whose sisters envy her. The fairy tale brings together natural and unnatural forces, and symbolizes, like many other fairy tales, the emergence of a modern human hero.

Whereas myths reflect the thinking of the people in the ancient world, where the connections between man and gods, fantasy and reality, one entity and another were less differentiated, Grimms' fairy tales, collected at the beginning of the nineteenth century, represent a different mode of thinking as well as a different worldview in which the emergence of the individual is evident and s/he becomes more differentiated: the individual psyche is coming to life and develops. Actually, in most fairy tales, the events of the tale begin when a problematic situation becomes unbearable for the heroine, forcing her to action. The heroine extracts herself from the problematic situation, usually within the family context, and begins a maturation–individuation process. Jacob Grimm viewed fairy tales as the remains of myths and, historically, they do represent a later product. The two sisters of Two-eyes represent a less differentiated level, reminding us of mythological figures. Indeed, One-eye, for example, is directly associated with the mythological one-eyed Cyclops. A trace of Three-eyes can be found in Japanese mythology, where creatures named Oni are depicted as being similar to humans, except that they usually have three eyes, big mouths, horns, and sharp nails. They also fly around and seize wicked souls on their deathbeds. Three-eyed creatures are certainly unnatural. The tale reflects the inner struggle between different forces dynamically active inside human beings. As Lévi-Strauss (1995) has pointed out, myth does not reveal how the man in the myth thinks but, rather, how the myth thinks in human beings. Comparing the above fairy tale to myths that include similar motives might help us understand the meaning of the eyes in the tale. One-eye and Three-eyes both represent a deviation from the usual order, thus breaking the *status quo*. The tale might actually portray the intense struggle between order and disorder, striving to achieve balance in a chaotic world. Lévi-Strauss writes (1995, p. 13), "since after all the human mind is only part of the universe, the need to find order probably exists because there is some order in the universe and the universe is not a chaos."

The fairy tale describes the passage between an ancient mode of life and a more developed, civilized one. If the tale begins with some kind of deficiency, lack, or crisis, forcing the hero to undertake a journey in order to repair this "initial situation" (Propp, 1968), the status at the end of the tale portrays a more advanced stage, sometimes even ripeness or fruitful perfection in the union achieved by the marriage of the hero and heroine. When the ancient creature is replaced by a more advanced one, envy of the one who takes its place certainly erupts. This explanation raises the question as to why the mother has two eyes. This case is similar to the Cinderella tale, in which, although the stepsisters are ugly in many versions, the evil mother is not necessarily ugly. Actually, in the popular Disney film, she appears as rather beautiful. We suggest that she represents culture and reality, with its restrains and limitation. This is why she is so evil to the heroine, who represents fantasy.

The struggle between different modes of life exists both in the development of human society and in the level of individual development, shifting from aggregation and massification to differentiation (Hopper, 2003b) as we can also see in large groups.

Tulips in return for eyes

We shall now compare the Grimm version with two Jewish parallels in which the eye is associated with envy. In both cases, the concrete events in the plot are bizarre and surreal. Deciphering the idiomatic expression hidden behind the concrete plot helps to reveal possible meanings of the tales. Whereas, in the Grimm version, the expressions related to the eyes are associated with watching and dealing with reality, the Jewish versions present a somewhat different situation: The first tale was told by Moshe Papo, who came to Israel from Bulgaria, and its number in IFA is 16243.

> "A widowed father, who had one daughter by his dead wife, remarried. The second wife also gave him one daughter. Her daughter always rested, and everybody spoiled her, while the stepdaughter had to wake up early, feed the chickens and clean the yard. Each morning, the girl washed the entrance of the house. Each morning, the prince went out on a trip, riding his horse with his servant. He realized that all the doorways of the other houses were dirty, except this house. One morning, he saw the girl and fell in love with her. He gave her his ring. After a while, the prince wanted to become engaged. He decreed that all seventeen-year-old girls should come to the court. The stepmother put very salty bread in their bag, and they went to the court. On their way, her daughter said, "I am so hungry." Her mother gave her bread that was not salty. When the stepdaughter asked for bread, the stepmother replied, "Give me one eye in return for the bread." She gave her an eye, and the stepmother gave her salty bread. The daughter asked for water, and in return she had to give her second eye. The stepmother pushed her out of the carriage in the middle of the journey. The daughter cried and cried, and did not know where she was. A shepherd who passed by took her to his house. He told his mother what happened. In the meanwhile, a rumour has been spread that the prince did not find the beloved girl and he became sick. The girl told the shepherd's mother the story about the ring, and the mother understood that it belonged to the prince. She cooked a soup and put the ring in it. The shepherd went to the king's court and asked to come in,

claiming that he could heal the sick prince. When he entered the prince's room, he gave him the soup. The prince felt the ring and asked where he got it from. The shepherd told him the story of the girl and promised to bring her sight back. He went away and picked tulips. After, he started selling the tulips in return for eyes. The daughter of the stepmother asked her mother to buy the tulips, as she did not need the extra eyes she got. They bought tulips for one eye, and the shepherd gave the eye to the girl. The same thing happened after a few days, and he took the second eye and gave it to the girl. Then, the girl and the prince got married, and everybody was happy".

Jasmine in return for eyes

The below IFA tale was told by Ziona Boaron, who came to Israel from Libya. Its number is 6710.

"Once there was a king who had three daughters. The oldest was too old for marriage, the middle one was ready to marry, and the third was young. None of them had ever known any man. An old woman heard about the three daughters and went to visit them, pretending to be their aunt. She asked them, 'How long will you remain without a groom?' and they replied, 'What should we do?' She advised them: 'Buy three melons: rotten, ripe, and unripe and give them to your father. He will understand the hint.' The daughters listened to her advice, but the king did not understand, until his servant explained to him that the rotten melon was his eldest daughter, the ripe was his middle one, and the unripe was the youngest. 'What should I do?' asked the king, and arranged a big feast. The eldest daughter started to choose her groom. She threw a golden apple that fell next to a prince, whom she married. The same happened to the middle daughter, but the apple of the youngest fell three times next to a baker, whom she finally married, suffering sorrow and misery. Before she gave birth to a baby, she went to visit her sisters, but they turned their backs on her, as they were afraid she would ask for some kind of favor. During the labor, a voice was heard through a violent storm, saying that she was just about to give birth to a magical girl, and that when the child cried, her tears would turn into pearls, her hair would turn into gold, and a jasmine would blossom in every step she took. And that is what happened. The family became rich; the name of the girl was known everywhere and the prince of Istanbul decided to marry her. He filled seven ships with gold and silver, and her mother agreed to the marriage. When he returned to Istanbul, he left a ship for the use of his future wife, together with an old woman to watch over her. But the old woman was mean. She starved the girl, and when she had no power at all and asked for something, the old woman replied, 'some food for an eye, some food for an eye'. The girl had no choice, and she gave the old woman one of her eyes. When the future wife asked for a drink, the woman said, 'water for an eye, water for an eye'. The girl gave her the second eye, and the old woman left her completely blind on a rock, and took her own daughter to the prince, to take the place of his wished-for wife.

"While the ship sailed toward the prince, two doves flew to the blind girl and fed her with vegetables that turned her into a dove. The dove flew to the prince's palace, and began to visit the prince's garden and eat from his fruit trees. One day, she was caught and put into a cage. The prince liked the dove and he took to her so much that he neglected his wife. Furthermore, no gold was produced out of his wife's hair, no pearls fell from her eyes, and no jasmine blossomed in her steps. The prince felt disappointed and deceived. The wife complained to her mother, and the old woman convinced the doctor to make the prince eat his beloved dove, and he did so. After the meal, the old woman threw away the dove's bones, and a wonderful apple tree grew out of her bones. The prince loved the apple tree. He took to it so much that he neglected his wife, who complained again. Her mother convinced the prince to uproot the tree, and give its fruit to his wife, and he did so. But a woman took the tree's trunk to her house. Every day, after she went out, a blind girl came out of the trunk and cleaned the house. One day, the woman discovered the blind girl, and adopted her as her own child. The girl told her about the cruel old woman. The good woman advised her, 'Gold is coming out of your hair and jasmine blooms wherever you step. Fill a basket with jasmine and go to sell it. Tell everybody: "jasmine for an eye, jasmine for an eye".' The girl followed her mother's advice. When she reached the palace, the mean old woman heard her, and gave her two eyes in return for two jasmines. The girl regained her sight. In those days, the prince gave cows to everyone, and declared that he who made his cow the fattest would receive a good price. The good woman made her cow very fat, and her adopted daughter brought the cow to the prince. The prince realized that jasmine bloomed wherever the girl stepped. He asked her, 'Where are you from, and where have you been?' and she told him everything. He ordered the mean old woman and her daughter to be killed, and married his true wife in a great feast. The cow's flesh was given to all the poor people who came to celebrate the happy wedding.

An eye for an eye

In Hebrew, as well as in many other languages, when we say "an eye for an eye" we mean revenge. In the Jewish Bulgarian tale, this idiomatic expression attains a concrete form. The origin of this expression is the Code of Hammurabi, a Babylonian law code of ancient Mesopotamia, dating back to about 1754 BC. It is one of the oldest deciphered writings in the world. One of the most famous laws in this code is, "If a man destroys the eye of another man, they shall destroy his eye". Hammurabi code was written a thousand years before the Bible was written, but its influence on the Jewish biblical law is astounding in both content and in style:

> And a man who inflicts an injury upon his fellow man just as he did, so shall be done to him [namely], fracture for fracture, eye for eye, tooth for tooth. Just as he inflicted an injury upon a person, so shall it be inflicted upon him. (Leviticus 24: 19–21)

It is possible that, as this code is found in several cultures, it reflects some deep "natural law" in the human mind.

Lévi-Strauss (1995) suggested that in order to understand the meaning of one myth, we should compare it to other myths. In order to understand the central role of the eye in the context of envy and greed, we shall turn to additional sources such as the oedipal myth. The poking out of the eye in the oedipal myth is associated with the emergence of consciousness. When people see or become aware of something beyond their capacity to tolerate, they sense it as dangerous. In the next chapter dealing with the blind king, we demonstrate the connection between seeing and knowing. The meaning of knowing in the Bible enables us to associate sight and eyes with love and sex. We fall in love with what we see, so poking out the eye prevents the person from falling in love. Many expressions about love are associated with seeing (such as "love at first sight"). We need the eyes in order to know something, and knowing in the Bible is physical.

Love in the fairy tales is primary love, like all the other experiences in this genre. This explains why, in different cultures and peoples, the eye connects with envy and greed. In all the above versions, the eye acquires a central function in the story, dealing with envy among sisters. Although the plots are different, the centrality of the eye is constant, and in all cases it happens in a strange, surreal way. A possible way of interpreting this strange act of poking out the eye is to decipher the idiomatic expression that is hidden behind the act. All of the above helps us to understand the experience of the eye in the social unconscious of different peoples. Other expressions in different languages validate these ideas, such as "big eyes" or "narrow eyes".

Linking the eye to revenge in different languages and cultures and its appearance in the folk tradition of different peoples is worth noting. In both the Grimms' and the Jewish versions, this revenge is also associated with envy. In Hebrew, the parallel expression for envy is "a narrow eye", and when we say "to poke out someone's eye", it means to make someone envious. The stepmother could not tolerate the heroine's good fortune, so she pokes her eyes out.

One main difference between the Jewish and the Grimms' versions is that the first were orally told and never appeared in print. These tales were transmitted in the family and society, from one generation to another, being orally preserved and used in order to illustrate scenes, conflicts, desires, and anxieties that could not be expressed publicly. The Grimms' version, although claimed to be based on folk tradition, has undergone the process of editing and publishing and, therefore, a higher degree of censorship is evident. In many of the Grimms' versions, the heroine who suffers misery and distress forgives her sisters in the end. This is a Christian motive of forgiveness and mercy. However, this is also a way to avoid aggression.

Among the psychoanalysts who acknowledged the centrality of envy and jealousy in human development, Klein (1984) and her work provide an important perspective in order to understand these powerful, fundamental experiences. The definition of envy used by Klein is the anger we experience when another person possesses and enjoys something desirable, often accompanied by an impulse to take it away or spoil it. She considers envy to be crucial in understanding both love and gratitude, and views it as a natural phase in human development. Klein thinks that envious impulses operate from the beginning of life, initially directed against the feeding breast and then against parental coitus. The attack on the good object leads to confusion between good and bad. She sees envy as a manifestation of primary destructiveness, to some extent constitutionally based, and worsened by adversity. Envy heightens persecution and guilt. Envy is an emotion that people do not want to own, although Klein describes it as a universal phenomenon and part of every human development. Thus, we can assume that it is part of the collective unconscious, attaining different modes in different societies.

In summary, envy can attain different national forms and it seems as if it had a special meaning in the foundation matrices of many societies, who were preoccupied with superiority and inferiority issues as part of establishing national identity. Apparently, in many cultures, the eye is unconsciously associated with envy and greed. In his famous play *Othello*, which is all about jealousy, Shakespeare (1988) labelled jealousy "the green eyed monster" (Iago: "Oh, beware, my lord, of jealousy! It is the green-eyed monster which doth mock the meat it feeds on" Act 3, Scene 3). This connection between envy and eyes can be decoded through deciphering the phenomenon of realizations of idiomatic expressions we find in fairy tales.

CHAPTER FIVE

"I (do not) see what you mean":
the concrete and metaphoric
dimensions of blindness in
fairy tales and the social mind*

Saramago's powerful novel *Blindness* (1997) uses blindness as a parable about society. People in his novel endure a plague that causes everyone to become blind. Losing their eyesight, they lose their humanity, and deteriorate to a complete loss of human dignity and basic values. The characters in the novel are subjected to virtually every form of human degradation: starvation, filth, rape, death, and horror are dispatched in daily and nightly allotments. All of this happens following the "white blindness" that is inflicted on the people. It seems that our ability to see is associated with feelings and morality accompanying humanity in general. However, we know that other species (actually most of the species, not necessarily human beings) are also capable of seeing. So, what is the difference? What are the various meanings of seeing in human life? And how is it that, in our daily language, *seeing* means *understanding*?

This chapter discusses various aspects of blindness and denial in human experience as reflected in different literary genres. Examining

---
* This chapter is based on Raufman & Weinberg (2014), published in *Group Analysis*, 47(2): 159–174.

expressions of blindness in the fairy tale genre helps us explore the concrete, somatic, primary dimension of the social mind. Examining a group workshop utilizing a short story (written by an individual author) in which blindness and denial play a central role helps us explore some abstract, artistic expressions of the foundation matrix of specific group members that are expressed at a more metaphorical level. The functions of blindness and denial in a short literary story are examined within the context of this bibliotherapuetic group workshop. Comparing this kind of narrative and group process to the ways in which blindness is described in the more social product, fairy tales, helps to shed light upon the relations between universal and more local aspects of blindness in the social unconscious, as well as between different levels of thought processes, both concrete and abstract. Increasing awareness and reducing denial (blindness) is of central importance in psychoanalysis and plays a central role in both individual and group psychotherapy. Therefore, we find the exploration of various aspects of blindness as reflected in artistic human works as carrying major significance.

Blindness in mythical thought and the social unconscious

The greatest Indian epical myth, the *Mahabharata*, uses the metaphor of blindness with a masterly skill (see Buck, 2000; Lothspeich, 2009). The story starts with Dhritarashtra and Pandu, who were sons of King Shantanu. Because Dhritarashtra was blind, Pandu became the king, though Dhritarashtra was the elder one. Only later, after Pandu's death, did Dhritarashtra take up kingship. The innermost narrative kernel of the *Mahabharata* portrays the story of the sons of the deceased King Pandu, the Pandavas, and the sons of blind King Dhritarashtra, the Kauravas, who became bitter rivals, and opposed each other in war. From a psychological perspective, we can talk about transgenerational transmission of sibling rivalry.

Having lost everything at some point of the plot, the Pandavas had to live in the forest for thirteen years. After those years, when they returned, they were refused their share of the kingdom. When all negotiations failed, the Pandavas decided that they had no choice but to declare war against the Kauravas. All the other kings and warriors, including the mutual relatives, elders, and friends of the Pandavas and Kauravas, joined one of the two camps. This can be seen as the result of a splitting mechanism in its utmost expression.

The Kauravas were all blinded by their ignoble passion of hatred, jealousy, and malice for the Pandavas. In their blindness, they brought upon themselves not only total ruin but also ignominy and effacement. Even the severe losses in the battlefield and the failure of their heinous crimes against the Pandavas failed to awaken them.

Dhritarashtra was born blind. Other heroes and heroines in the story chose to be blind for various reasons. Here are some examples: Kandhari, by bandaging her eyes, perhaps out of unconscious knowledge of not being a witness to the disastrous, tragic fall-out of the blindness of all in her family and around her; Shakuni was blinded by his total hatred for the Pandavas, inventing and conceiving every tactic of the intellect to engulf everybody in his venomous plots. Duryodhana, fed and inflamed by Shakuni, was blinded by his towering ambition to be the supreme ruler of the kingdom.

On the Western side of the globe, the great Greek mythical play *Oedipus Rex* uses blindness as a metaphor as well. Sight does not come with a mere set of eyes. Throughout the play, a sightless man sees all and a man who is rich with vision sees nothing of his own life. We understand it by contrasting the blind seer, Teiresias, with Oedipus, who is blind to his own actions and his eventual sight of the truth: "... You mock my blindness, do you? / But I say that you, with both your eyes, are blind" (Sophocles, 400–401). The very first example of the continuous metaphor of blindness is seen at the beginning through the old, physically blind Teiresias. After being sent to speak of what he knows of the murder of the King, he reveals that it is Oedipus who has, indeed, killed the king. Oedipus, on the other hand, blindly denies this fact. He does not, even for a second, entertain the idea that the old man might have some truth to his tale. Even after learning that the king was killed in the same way Oedipus had admitted to killing an unknown man, and many other bits of information that point the finger towards him, he still remains blind to the fact that he is the murderer.[19]

As both Eastern and Western great myths use blindness as a metaphor for denial and psychological avoidance of truth, it is possible that it has similar universal meanings which is probably rooted in the social or collective unconscious.

According to Weinberg's (2007) definition of the social unconscious, myths are included, and fairy tales can reveal a lot about myths in a certain society. We do not claim that myths and fairy tales are unconscious, but, rather, conscious products that may express, reflect, and echo some unconscious dimension in an indirect way and help to integrate these two estranged divisions of the mind.

As mentioned in our introduction, in many cases, idiomatic expressions are the fairy tale's way to describe emotions, dynamics, and complex ideas that cannot be described literally, in its own unique language, as this genre is located on the borderline between the realms of the concrete and the abstract. In some cases, the idiomatic expression may echo experiences that emerge from the most primary levels of mental organization.

We will now examine how the realization of idiomatic expression appears in a fairy tale, providing the psychological experience of blindness in a concrete, somatic form, by discussing a specific case of Iraqi–Jewish folk tradition. We shall demonstrate how a realization of an idiomatic expression appearing in this tale might testify to issues related to the social unconscious of this ethnic community, as well as to the social unconscious in a more collective, universal manner.

"The Wonderful Leaves": the king becomes blind

Below is a shortened version of the tale "The Wonderful Leaves" (this tale is recorded in the Israeli Folktale Archive, IFA, located in the University of Haifa).

> Once there was a king and queen. They had three daughters. The king wanted his daughters to marry rich men from the upper class. Indeed, the eldest daughter was married to a prince, as was the second daughter. The youngest daughter, however, preferred to marry her beloved man, who was poor. The king objected to this marriage and banished his daughter from the palace. She married her poor husband and they lived in poverty, but with joy and happiness. After that, the king became blind, and no doctor could cure him. One day, he met a doctor who said, "There is one special tree, whose leaves may cure the king's blindness. The king called his two rich sons-in-law, asking them to go on a quest for the wonderful leaves, but they failed to complete the mission. Only the youngest daughter's husband was brave enough to

overcome all the obstacles, bring the leaves and cure the king. The king banished his older sons-in-law, appointed the youngest to be his deputy, and they all lived happily ever after.

Thirteen parallels of this tale-type can be found in the IFA, emerging from Morocco, Tunisia, Yemen, Iraq-Kurdistan, Persia-Kurdistan, Afghanistan, and India. The main motif in our version, which also exists in all of the IFA versions with no exception, is the sudden and inexplicable blindness of the king. This blindness appears in the tale as a concrete event, describing eyes that cannot see. Exposing the metaphorical meaning of the concept "blind", which refers to the inability to see things in a clear and realistic manner, helps to establish the connection between both levels, abstract and concrete, which are personified and embodied in the figure of the king. This type of explanation helps to understand the event of suddenly becoming blind and the way it is perceived in the social unconscious of the communities that preserve this kind of story. Apparently, this event appears in the story in an arbitrary, unexplained, and detached manner. The idiom "blind" (in its metaphoric meaning) exists in many languages, whereas "seeing" means "understanding" ("I see what you mean").

The king is blind to the situation

At the beginning of the tale, we are informed of the king's opposition to his youngest daughter's desire to marry a poor man. As a result, she is banished from the kingdom. This opening presents one of the central conflicts in the tale, which deals with the following question: What is more important in life, external characteristics *vs.* internal ones, or, more specifically, money and status *vs.* inner virtues and personal characters. The act of banishing expresses the king's inability to welcome something deviant, and, thus, unacceptable, into his existential worldview. This kind of thinking might be associated with primary levels of mental organization (in both the individual and the social mind) as it prioritizes things that can be actually seen over internal, abstract values. This challenge threatens the king, requires a special effort, and demands an elaboration and articulation of his behavior. The fairy tale genre, as it expresses archaic modes of thinking in the social unconscious, tends to present its figures in a somewhat simplistic manner, one in which they cannot bear, or cope with, complexity. However, this banishment is a solution that "suffers" from blindness. The king's psychological blindness immediately attains a concrete translation when he actually becomes blind after banishing his daughter, with no clear explanation given for this blindness. His blindness appears right after the act of banishment, as an immediate response to the king's behavior. This is the fairy tale's primary way of expressing mental ideas in a somatic, concrete form. As the king's psychological blindness is expressed in the decisions he makes relating to the youngest groom, it is not surprising that only the youngest groom can cure the king's concrete blindness by acquiring the wonderful leaves. Only when the youngest groom is finally recognized as an important contribution to the family by exhibiting courage and determination can he then "open the king's eyes". The king finally realizes the youngest groom's worthiness and the full value of the marriage. The youngest groom opens the king's eyes on the metaphoric level—by making the king view him as a favored groom. At the same time, he opens the king's eyes on the concrete level when he actually cures his blinded eyes, making him see again.

This example demonstrates the way in which the idiomatic expressions "like a blind person" (in the spoken language of the Iraqi Jews), "being blind to the situation" or—with an opposite meaning—"to see the situation" (which exactly describes the king's existential position and includes sensorial experience), in the fairy tale achieve realization. Exposing this mechanism illustrates the different layers of thinking that function in the tale, while the metaphorical expression ("being blind") does not appear in the tale on the overt level. Instead, it must be extricated from the concrete level of acts taking place in the narrative.

The king cannot "see" his daughter

When we say that we "see" the other, we usually mean that we understand the other person at a deep level: We understand their needs, we acknowledge their subjectivity, we "know" them on an intimate level. This is the way that an ideal mother "sees" her baby: She understands him without words identifying his needs and is ready to acknowledge those needs and also to respond to them many times. In a way, this is the romantic infantile fantasy of any intimate relationship: we want the other to "see" us. Not to "hear" us, but to see us without words and without making the adult effort of communicating our needs.

In therapy, this hidden deep wish is evoked frequently in the transference relationship: Our need to be seen by the therapist can be enacted, especially in places that our parents or caretakers failed to see us. Whereas different schools of psychoanalysis developed different concepts and techniques to deal with this need (usually by interpreting and frustrating it), the concept of empathy developed by Kohut (1977) seems to have a special contribution, especially by shifting the therapist's emphasis from interpretation to seeing the patient from a close veiwpoint. Self-psychology emphasizes empathy and the ability to "see" and acknowledge the patient's needs.

In a group therapy session, one member showed up quite late. When he entered the room, he said nothing. The group was in the middle of an important discussion and the members continued exploring the issue in which they were immersed. After a few minutes, the latecomer could not tolerate it any more and exploded: "I am so angry and frustrated! You do not care that my car broke down on the way here, and I had to wait for the mechanic to come and fix it. You do not appreciate the efforts that I've made to come to the group tonight." Apparently, he was sure that the group could, and should, see and understand him without his explaining himself.

"I see you" is the official theme song from the science fiction film *Avatar* (2009), in which the native tribe of the Na'vi lives in the alien world of Pandora. They appear primitive, but, in fact, are highly evolved. *Avatar's* Na'Vi subscribe to a combination of pantheism and theism. They have an experience of unity of consciousness with other beings, all of which are really just manifestations of one Being. "I see you" is a greeting in the Na'vi language. Furthermore, the Na'vi have two versions of the verb *see*: *tse'a*, which pertains to physical vision and *kame*, which means to see in a spiritual sense. It is more closely a synonym of "understand", or "comprehend". "To see" is a cornerstone of Na'vi philosophy. It is to open the mind and heart to the present, and embrace Pandora as if encountering it for the very first time.

In the above fairy tale, the king cannot "see" his daughter. He does not see her needs and confuses his values, interests, and needs with hers. He is not interested in understanding her in the deep sense, or to learn why she chose that poor husband and not a rich, high-society man. The tale describes no dialogue between the king/father and his daughter, as it is not important for the king to know and understand his daughter's motives and inner world, but to force her to obey his wishes and needs. The king is blind to who his daughter is.

Blindness in other literary works

Whereas the way in which blindness is expressed in the fairy tale genre helps to shed light upon issues related to the primary levels of the collective unconscious, the example we present now teaches about different aspects related to the functions of blindness in both the foundation matrix of a certain group, and in a group process.

The vignette presented below is taken from a group process with Israeli students studying bibliotherapy. It exemplifies some of the roles of blindness in human experience. In this workshop, group members were requested to choose a short story and bring it to class, while the other students were invited to share their associations, thoughts, and feelings, evoked by that story. One of the students chose to bring the story "The Berries' Girl", written by the Israeli writer Savion Librecht (1992). This story is told from the point of view of a German woman, a Nazi officer's wife, who lives with her husband (who serves as the vice-commander of a concentration camp) and her child in the officers' compound on the outskirts of one of the concentration camps in Poland during the Second World War. The woman describes a Jewish girl who brings huge, beautiful, tasty berries to the officers' wives. The girl grows these berries in the camp, and, at the end of the story, it is revealed that she grew them on the ashes of the Jews exterminated in the crematorium.

The storyteller is bunkered in her own world and is blind to the real situation and atrocities around her. She convinces herself that the smoky chimneys behind the wall belong to a factory in which the prisoners are working. Up until the end of the story, when the family returns to Germany, she remains blind to the situation and keeps denying the truth of what is actually happening beyond the wall. Unlike the Nazi's wife, the readers know the truth about the atrocities and why the girl looked so shabby and suffered from malnutrition.

It was fascinating to see what happened when this story was brought into the group of Israeli students, and how this woman's blindness illuminated aspects in the awareness of the participants in the group. We will not describe the entire deep and complicated process that occurred in the group when the story was told, but, rather, focus on the issue of blindness. The students' experience was so extreme that the one who brought the story felt guilty for bringing this difficult text. While the fictional storyteller was naïve, guilt-free, and blind, ignoring any sound or smell, the group reacted with heightened senses. Two of the group participants felt nausea as a response to the eating of the berries by the officers' wives. It seems that while those wives in the story, in order to continue to live normally on the border of the concentration camp, developed a kind of a stupor, a "blindness" toward the terrible reality that prevented any nausea or shock, these feelings, through projective identification, were deposited in the readers. The group participants allowed themselves to feel what the teller in the story could not let herself feel or be in touch with. The group members created a dialogue with the text that completed the missing parts in the point of view of the protagonist who told the story.

Zoran (2000) reminds us that although the literary text is not a human being, it may serve as a self-object. Readers create transference responses while interacting with literary texts like any other human interaction. While in the fictitious world of the text, the blindness functions as a salient mechanism; it works as an illuminating force in the world outside the text. We can learn from this dynamic something important about blindness and its role in society. The main process accompanying the experience resulted not only in increasing of (in)sight, but also in expressing the conflict between the need to see, the need to not see, to blur, "to become blind". The guilt feeling of the student who brought the text to the group expressed several issues: It echoed the question of guilt related to the events in the story in general, but, more specifically, he felt guilty for "illuminating the eyes" of the participants, or perhaps introducing/instilling into their awareness content that is too difficult and horrific, to the point that it is better to ignore or repress it. In confirmation, some of the participants admitted that they cannot read "Holocaust stories".

As part of the Israeli social unconscious (Weinberg, 2017), for more than two decades after the Second World War (in the 1950s and 1960s), the Holocaust was not deeply discussed in Israeli society, and people could not listen to the stories of the survivors and acknowledge their horrible experiences, resulting in transgenerational transmission of trauma from Holocaust survivors to the second generation (Wardi, 1992). The Holocaust, as one of the major Israeli social traumas, had been perceived for years as a deep threat to the young Israeli society, which was preoccupied with building a new country and society. From the other side of the coin, as Wilke has noted (2007), the German society used its own denial and repression, and the second generation of Nazi children, because of shame and disappointment, could not process the atrocities carried out by their parents. The second generation of Second World War Germans could not ask their fathers: "Daddy, what did you really do in the war?" Actually, the story describes exactly this kind of denial and blindness from the German side, as Wilke concludes: "Second generation perpetrator children in groups have a need to work on the level of the individual as well as the social unconscious" (2007, p. 445).

In the Israeli group process, choosing this story was a call to wake up from the denial and repression related to the Holocaust, despite the guilt it might evoke. The student who brought the story to the group is a child of Holocaust survivors. His most fundamental childhood memories are associated with this existential fact. Therefore, he had a real dilemma about whether to bring the story to the group or not. He tried avoiding the role, the one he felt he always served, of the second generation of Holocaust survivors. On the other hand, he felt that not choosing this text would be a kind of ignoring and denying his authentic needs. This conflict is not only a personal individual issue, but is also part of the Israeli unconscious.

Blindness, psychotherapy, and the social unconscious

In clinical terms, therapy aims to increase "sight" (awareness). The difficulty begins when the need to see contradicts the need not to see—to repress, deny, and reject. The dialogue occurring around the text "The Berries' Girl" reflected this struggle existing not only in the individual mind, but also in the group mind and, perhaps, in the social mind (or social unconscious).

Attaining knowledge is crucial for human development, and obstacles to achieving knowing are addressed in all cultures. Ignoring truth is one of these obstacles. Group analysis is also interested in increasing participants' awareness and making unconscious issues (whether social or personal) more conscious through mirroring, resonance, and other group processes.

Although Aristotle (1991) declared (in *The Metaphysics*, 350 BCE) "all men by nature desire to know", in 1912, Ferenczi pointed out the human desire not to know, which is constantly in conflict with the desire to know (Ferenczi, 1950). Bion (1959) claimed that the human need to think and to know conflicts with a desire to avoid the mental pain that accompanies gaining knowledge. Knowing oneself (and the world) can be confusing, anxiety provoking, and disturbing. Group analysis attempts to create and sustain a group culture in which members explore the truth and seek knowledge. However, when anxiety intensifies, defense mechanisms are at work and the group becomes blind, using denial excessively. As we have seen, this struggle between knowledge and blindness is reflected in many myths and folk tales.

The use of the metaphor of eyes and sight is ubiquitous. The common proverb says, "The eyes are the mirror of the soul". A person's inner world, one's feelings and experiences, are seen, perceived, and reflected through the eyes of the observer. So, the eyes are an entrance connecting inner and outer reality, like a gate through which important emotional material passes.

Psychotherapy is about opening one's eyes to truth by working through defense mechanisms such as denial and repression. Classical psychoanalysis was based around the myth of Oedipus, mentioned above, who blinded himself after recognizing the truth about his having murdered his father and slept with his mother. This act can be understood, among many other interpretations (e.g., guilt) as a metaphor for his own blindness, ignoring the clear signs that he is committing sins. Paradoxically, examining the plot, it seems as if the blind is the only one with true (in)sight. Group analysis is also about "enlightening" group members, opening their eyes and increasing their awareness, not only to their own personal unconscious, but to the social unconscious as well.

However, we also need to remember that "seeing" the truth, or perceiving reality, is more complicated, and there are aspects of reality that can be "seen" while we can be blind to other perspectives. This complexity can be deduced from the famous fable about the blind men and the elephant: It is a Hindu story of a group of blind men who touch an elephant to learn what it is like. Each one feels a different part, such as the tusk or the trunk. When each describes his own reality, they learn that they are in complete disagreement. So what is truth?

CHAPTER SIX

"To step into someone's shoes": the tales about Cinderella

> "Give a girl the right shoes, and she can conquer the world"
> (Marilyn Monroe, www.brainyquote.com/
> quotes/keywords/shoes.html)

Recently, a colleague shared with us an activity he conducts in his therapy groups in which group members are invited to take off their shoes and locate them in the room as a sociometric exercise. During this activity in one of the groups, a participant put her foot into another group member's shoe. Later, she felt embarrassed and ashamed. Understanding her behavior as a realization of the idiomatic expression "to step into someone's shoes" allows us to interpret her act as a manifestation of empathy: Entering her group mate's shoe puts her in his position. However, if this was the case, why should she feel embarrassed? Actually, the participant who owned the shoe was the only male member in the group. Later, in the group discussion, this female participant shared that her association to this behavior related to sexuality—a topic that was further processed in the group. We will not elaborate here on the group vignette, which was quite vivid and passionate. Rather, we use this example to reflect on the role that shoes (or, more precisely, a foot entering a shoe) play in the human experience, especially the relationship between the sexes regarding issues of uniqueness, exclusiveness, and matching. One cannot avoid comparing this group vignette to the famous Cinderella tale in which the matching between one particular foot and one unique shoe is of central importance.

This chapter deals with one of the most popular and widespread fairy tales, *Cinderella*. Even though the various versions of this tale type differ from one another in so many aspects, the shoe motif, in which the heroine is the only one to fit a certain unique shoe and, therefore, the only one who can marry the prince (motif H36.1 in the Thompson motifs index), remains relatively stable. Most of the Cinderella tales include an idiomatic expression that attains a concrete, visual form and is part of the daily language of many different peoples. We are talking about the idiom "to step into someone's shoes" which may appear in many different versions, such as "try to walk a mile in my shoes", "to fill one's shoe", "to enter one's shoes" and so forth.

The way in which this idiom attains a concrete pictorial form in the Cinderella tale is a precise translation of the abstract metaphoric idea that no one can get into the heroine's shoe—no other maiden in the entire kingdom can take her place. The ability to get into someone's shoes may be understood in several ways. For example, in some languages it means being empathic. When we get into the other's shoe, or "walk a mile in his or her shoe" we know something about how it feels to be him or her. In some languages, when we enter too big shoes it means that we are challenged to take the place of another individual and are expected to fulfill high standards and expectations. Following this idea, it is interesting that, in some versions of the Cinderella tale, the maidens in the kingdom need to have a small enough foot to fit the shoe, and not a big one. This can be understood in the light of social and cultural aspects, taking into consideration the social status of women and the idea that a small foot is associated with tenderness and gentleness. However, many versions of this tale type do not necessarily present a small shoe, but, rather, a unique one which fits only one foot in the entire kingdom. Whereas different interpretations suggest viewing this resemblance between a certain shoe and a certain foot on the symbolic level (see, for example, Nacht, 1915), following our methodology we suggest understanding this concrete plot detail, that no other maiden can fit into Cinderella's shoe, as a realization of the idiomatic expression. This plot detail is so prevalent and it is rare to find a version of this tale type around the world that does not include it. In addition, this plot detail always appears in a context of a unique maiden that no one can take her place.

We can see how the symbolic interpretation is in line with our model, as it deals with uniqueness and a total match between one particular foot and one particular shoe and, therefore, between one particular woman and one particular man. However, exposing this phenomenon enables us to view the relations in the Cinderella tale in a more complicated manner and to shed additional light on the subject of marital exclusiveness. Before discussing the possible meanings of this motif and the realization of the idiomatic expression involved in this plot detail, we should briefly review the famous and less famous versions of this tale-type existing around the world.

The Cinderella versions

The Cinderella tale is one of the most popular fairy tales in both Western and non-Western cultures. It is rare to find a country, nation, or society that does not tell this story, or a collection of fairy tales from which this tale is absent. This wide distribution testifies to the relevance of this narrative for people from different cultures and societies and raises the need to explore its affinity to social issues—both conscious and unconscious. Tales similar to *Cinderella* exist in Chinese, Indian, African, Javanese, Australian, Japanese, and other peoples' folk literature. Its relevance is also evident in the fact that the tale has been adapted to the stage, film, television, and other media. As the Cinderella narrative is one of the most popular and famous fairy tales in the world, it has merited numerous studies adopting various approaches. Among the classics are the works of Marian Roalfe Cox (1893), the Swedish folklorist Anna Brigitta Rooth (1951), and Antti Aarne and Stith Thompson (1961). In the Aarne–Thompson classification index, this tale type is classified as AT 510, which includes the persecuted heroine, the magical help, the meeting with the prince, the identity proof, and the marriage to the prince. In the introduction to his collection of articles on *Cinderella*, Dundes (1982) compares the kinds of sub-types established by Cox, Rooth, and Aarne and Thompson.

Some attribute the origin of this fairy tale to China. A Chinese version dated from the ninth century tells a story about a heroine named Yeh-Shen, the daughter of a cave chief named Wu, who was raised by her evil stepmother after her real mother passed away. Yeh-Shen owned a magical fish that helped her to go to the spring festival. Although this version is full of unique Chinese characteristics, it also includes the motif in which the heroine leaves behind one of her golden slippers when she dashes out of the festival. She keeps the other slipper, by which the king recognizes her and marries her. The stability of this motif over the generations, in a way that crosses time and space, is impressive.

One of the most popular versions is the one written by Charles Perrault, first published anonymously in 1697 in Paris. Its popularity could be attributed to the Disney film based on this version. Because of its popularity, people are accustomed to thinking that the Cinderella tale always includes the tiny glass slipper, the fairy godmother, and the magical coach. However, this literary artistic version differs from the folk versions in many ways. Similar European tales are found in Bonaventure des Periers's *New Recreations and Joyous Games* (1843) and Giambattista Basile's *Pentamerone* (1932), in which the name of the heroine is Zezula. The Grimm version (*Aschenputtel*), first published in 1812, presents the magical transformations quite differently, but the shoe motif is presented in exactly the same way. This is also true for other versions presented in the popular printed collections. The shoe itself can be described in many different forms. For example, whereas the Perrault version describes a glass slipper, the Grimms' version, as well as one of the Chinese versions, include a golden shoe/slipper. Basile's Italian version describes a shiny shoe, and a Scottish version features a shoe made of expensive Atlas fabric. Many Jewish versions include a silver slipper and other versions present several different options, such as a shoe made of fur, silk, or velvet. Sometimes, the narrative does not provide a specific description of the shoe, but says merely that the shoe is unique and no other maiden in the entire kingdom except the heroine can fit into it.

The shoe motif dates back to ancient Greco-Egyptian times. *Rhodôpis* is an ancient tale about a Greek courtesan who marries the king of Egypt. The story was first recorded by the Greek historian Strabo in the first century BC (Green, 2011). The origins of the fairy tale's figure can be traced back to the sixth century BC *Hetaera*

Rhodopis (Herodotus (1937), *The Histories*, book 2, chapters 134–135). The story tells of an eagle that snatched one of Rhodopis's shoes from her maid while she was bathing. The eagle carried it to Memphis, and dropped it into the lap of the king (named Psammetichus). The king searched for the owner of the shoe. He found Rhodopis in Naucratis and married her.

A sub-type of the Cinderella tale, classified as AT510B in the Aarne-Thompson classification index, presents a different narrative in which the real mother, on her deathbed, makes a wish for the father to marry only the one to which her dress/ring fits. Unfortunately, her own daughter is the only one to meet this criterion and she is forced to marry her own father (motif S322.1.2). This sub-type covers several different tales, such as *Donkey Skin* (see Chapter Three about the Skin-Ego), *Catskin*, or *Cap o'Rushes* and has undergone several research investigations (Goldberg, 1997; Marshal, 2004; Muhawi, 2001; Nicolaisen, 1993). Goldberg (1997, p. 28) mentions three different sub-types: One is the Donkey Skin (Catskin, Cap o' Rushes) tale with beautiful dresses, parties, and a token of recognition. In another, known in Italy, Sudan, India, New Guinea, and Japan, the heroine wears a human skin and is discovered as she bathes. In the third, she hides inside a piece of furniture. For many reasons, these sub-types deserve a separate discussion. However, in the current context, it is worth noting that in most versions of these sub-types, the shoe motif still appears, even in cultures in which shoes are considered as a sign of inferiority, a symbol for dirtiness and insult, such as Muslim societies.

Muslim versions

Muhawi investigated Arab versions of this sub-type, both oral and printed, focusing on the representations of women's bodies. He explores the cultural significance of disguise in terms of identity and representation, comparing the Arab versions (Palestinian and Sudanese, named *Sackcloth, Fatma the Beautiful and the Son of Nimer*) with the Grimm ones (Grimm, num. 21: *Aschenputtel* and 65: *Allerleirauh*).

Muhawi emphasizes the differences that make up a local version, and, therefore, better enable us to study the relationship of the tales to culture. Since the subject of his study is an oral genre narrated in a local dialect or regional variety rather than written in standard Arabic, his analysis draws on areas of experience more closely allied to "folk" practices and beliefs than those belonging to the "elite" world of literate learning. However, alongside the investigation of the uniqueness of any local version, it is interesting to find the repetitive shoe motif appearing over and over again.

Some Jewish versions originating from Islamic countries present a cruel, lecherous father who wishes to marry his own daughter, not necessarily due to his wife's dying wish, but, rather, because of his own perverse desires. In the Uther classification index (2004), this subtype is classified as ATUB*, in which the father's sin is emphasized with no attempt to sublimate it or present him as a loyal husband to his wife. Bettelheim (1976) also points out that in many versions, the heroine escapes from her father who wishes to marry her. He mentions that this plot is prevalent in countries such as France, Italy, Austria, Greece, Ireland, Scotland, Poland, Russia, and Scandinavia. In other versions, her father exiles her because she does not love him as much as he does her. All these examples reveal how the Cinderella tales are much more complicated than can be seen at first glance. As the shoe motif is repetitive, we should use it in order to shed light on some of the complications, especially those associated with sexual relations and uniqueness/exclusiveness/possessiveness.

More than fifty variants of *Cinderella* are recorded in the Israeli Folktale Archive, most of which originate from Islamic countries. As noted above, even in Arab culture, in which shoes are considered as dirty, symbolizing inferiority, the shoe motif is still evident, in a very similar way to its appearance in Western societies. Some current examples taken from daily blogs and posts on the internet demonstrate the role shoes play in everyday life. On December 14, 2008, Muntadar al-Zeidi threw his shoes at the then US president, George W. Bush, shouting, "This is a farewell kiss from the Iraqi people, you dog." In an article posted on 15 December 2008, Gammell discusses this event. She writes,

> The shoe is considered dirty because it is on the ground and associated with the foot, the lowest part of the body. Hitting someone with a shoe shows that the victim is regarded as even lower. When Saddam Hussein's statue was toppled in Baghdad in April 2003, Iraqis swarmed around it, striking it with their shoes . . .

As an insult to President George Bush Snr after the first Gulf war, a mosaic of his face was laid on the floor of the Al-Rashid Hotel in Baghdad. Anyone who entered the lobby would have to walk over his face to get into the hotel.

She further writes that

> The shoe is such an offensive symbol that it is seen as culturally rude to cross an ankle over a knee and display the sole of the shoe while talking to another person.
>
> The shoe is also considered unclean in the Muslim faith and believers must remove them before prayers.

This is only one example out of many others, demonstrating the meaning of shoes in Arab culture.

So, how should we understand the fact that, in spite of this cultural meaning, the shoe motif in the Arab *Cinderella* versions remains loyal to its international counterpart, including Western versions, in which the shoe carries different meanings? The theoretical perspective adopted here enables us to view the shoe motif in the light of primary sensorial processes that govern human experience before the individual is exposed to cultural aspects. The experience of the match between one particular foot and one particular shoe is a physical experience that carries important implications, such as the ability to walk safely and, therefore, to achieve destinations, the feeling of being held and protected, and the basic sense of being in the right place. Anyone who has ever tried to walk in a shoe that does not fit knows something about the difficulties, discomfort, and pain involved in such an attempt.

Jewish versions

Israeli scholars have already discussed the unique characteristics of some of the Jewish versions of tale-type ATU 510A (Alexander, 1994; Bar-Itzhak, 1993). These considerations examined non-western versions (Moroccan and Yemen) in an Israeli context, emphasizing the oedipal component of the tales, among other features. Some of the versions belong to tale-type AT 510B (dress of gold, of silver, and of stars) in which the heroine is forced to marry her own father (discussed above). In some versions of this sub-type, there is an alteration of the shoe and the ring test for marriage with the father. Dundes (1987b, p. 60) views this alteration as a fine illustration for what has been termed the symbolic equivalent of allomotifs (p. 61): There is abundant independent evidence supporting the female genitals symbolism of both shoes and rings. Both are placed upon external appendages such as feet and fingers and can serve as metaphorical microcosms for heterosexual coitus. One thinks of the custom cited by Jones (1965) of throwing an old slipper or shoe after the departing newlywed couple with the explicit accompanying saying: may you fit her as well as my foot fits this old shoe. In most of the Cinderella versions, oral as well as printed, Western as well as non-Western, this idiom attains a concrete form in a way that can testify to the affinity between concrete and abstract modes of thinking in the minds of many peoples and cultures. This fact hints at the primary modes of thinking operating in the genre and is, therefore, manifested in a cross-cultural manner. It also enables understanding of the embarrassment of the female group member mentioned at the beginning of this chapter when she mistakenly entered the male's shoe.

Some of the versions of sub-type AT 510B are actually a conglomerate, combining characteristics belonging to another tale-type: *The Maiden Without Hands* (AT 706). As mentioned in Chapter Two, "ask for her hand", in this book, Dundes (1987b) reviews some of these versions, such as Romanian versions, which are representative: "on her death bed an empress told her husband, the emperor, that if he marries again he should take for his wife only the woman whose foot fitted into her shoe" (p. 60). After long years of search, the daughter, who had meanwhile grown up, chanced to put the shoe on. On discovering that, the emperor decided to marry her. The girl flees, but later the father finds her in the forest, where he cuts off her hands and nose and leaves her to her fate. The incestuous meanings of this tale-type have been discussed in many other places. However, in the current context, it is interesting to note the wide range of variations in which matching a foot and a shoe serves to demonstrate the idea of exclusiveness and possessiveness.

This is also evident in other sub-types of Cinderella, such as those in which the heroine is actively participating in her mother's death. For example, a Jewish Yemen story, titled *Haninat Alla*, tells of a heroine who is actively participating in her mother's murder. This heroine is very different from most of the European heroines, who are portrayed as innocent, helpless, and kind. Instead, she is determined, sophisticated, and vindictive. However, in many senses, the narrative keeps the familiar pattern of the international tale-type as well as the shoe motif. In this version, as in most of the others, the heroine loses her shoe while running away from the ball. When the prince looks for the maiden who owns the shoe, she is the only one who fits it. This is of special significance: in spite of the heroine being portrayed so differently from one version to another, the shoe motif remains relatively stable. What we get is a realization of the idiomatic expression "no one can fit into her shoe". The uniqueness of the heroine is still valid, even in cases in which she is a murderer.

This Jewish version originates from an Islamic country, Yemen, in which the shoe is an inferior object as well. Other versions that present a similar situation also emerge from Islamic countries such as Morocco. Various proverbs and idioms existing in different languages of Jews who live in Islamic countries exemplify this fact. For example, Iraqi Jews used to say: *"Ma Talbasu Be'Riglach"* ("May you put it on your foot"). People used to say it about an inferior person who deserves an attitude of disrespect, and whom they wished to be "like the despised shoe". An unimportant person is considered *Hada Kondra* ("equal to shoes"): not important and undeserving of any attention.[20] Among Yemenite Jews, from which the above version is taken, the shoe attains a similar status and this is also true for other Arab countries. Using the shoe as a test for proving the heroine's identity and the inability of all the other women in the kingdom to fit into the her shoe are, therefore, a precise translation of the metaphoric idiom "to step into someone's shoes", or, more precisely, "no one can enter her shoe". The example taken from the above Jewish Yemenite version demonstrates how the phenomenon of realization of idiomatic expressions is a cross-cultural one. Other languages have their own variants of this idiomatic expression. In English, it is common to say "to step into someone's shoes". Spanish people say *entrar en loss zapatos a genos*, meaning: "to get into others' shoes".[21] The complete match between the metaphoric meaning of the idiomatic expression that is realized in the tale and the existential situation of the heroine, in all versions, demonstrates the fairy tale's illustrative way to figuratively portray an abstract idea: In this case, the idea of the exclusive relations between a certain man and a certain woman.

Another Jewish Moroccan tale recorded in the IFA presents a similar synopsis:

> A woman had one son and one daughter. A widowed neighbour inflamed the girl against her mother and convinced her to murder her. The widowed father married the neighbor who had her own seven daughters and she mistreated the heroine, slandered her, blamed her for doing dirty things, and locked her in the baking room. Time passes, and the king's son announces that he is looking for a wife. The father of the unlucky girl brought her seven nuts.
>
> When the stepmother prevented the heroine from going to the ball by ordering her to fulfill impossible missions, a magic helper, named Samsam-Kamkam came out of the nut, turned her into a charming girl and carried her to the wedding feast, in which the prince fell for her.
>
> On her way back she lost one shoe. No other girl had a shoe like that, and who should find it but the king's son, who announced that only the one whom this shoe fits, would marry the prince.
>
> The heroine was the only one to fit the shoe, married the prince, and became pregnant. The father's wife envied the girl. She threw her into a well and disguised one of her own daughters as the prince's wife. In the meanwhile, the heroine's brother sat by the well and talked to his sister until the king's son passed by, found her, and saved her.

Here, again, we see how the shoe motif remains stable in a tale designed very differently than the classic familiar European versions. Many local characteristics are evident in the Moroccan version, such as the special food, the language, and other features that enable us to learn about the habits, customs, and norms of the society that tells and preserves this story. However, it seems that linking the shoe with matters of exclusiveness carries universal meanings. A Muslim Persian version collected by Mills (1982) in Iran, and which she claims is characteristic of both Iran and Afghanistan, contains narrative stages similar to those found in the Jewish Moroccan versions: an opportunistic teacher at a religious school questions one of her students, the daughter of a trader about her family's financial status. When the widowed teacher discovers that the family is well-off, she asks the girl what provisions they have at home. The girl tells her they have vinegar, whereupon the widow convinces her student of her good intentions and that the girl's mother is wicked. She then suggests that the girl should ask her mother to get her some vinegar, and that she should push her mother into the vessel in which the vinegar is stored and close it. The girl does so, and after some time the father marries the schoolteacher.

When the teacher has a daughter of her own, she begins to mistreat her stepdaughter. From that point on, the narrative follows the familiar synopsis of Cinderella, with the shoe serving as an identity test.

As Bar-Yitzhak (1993) has already pointed out, these versions may reinforce Bettelheim's suggestion regarding the oedipal components in the narrative. In this light, the humiliation and persecution of the heroine might be understood as a punishment for her murderous desires. Nonetheless, whether viewing the incest component in the narrative as oedipal desires, or as a real incest in the family, resulting from a patriarchal situation with a cruel, selfish father (as we shall soon present, in some versions emerging from Islamic countries), linking the shoe with sexual relations is evident, as well as a symbol for exclusiveness which may be understood in different contexts: As a sign of uniqueness, or, rather, possessiveness, depending on the social situation.

Gender, power, and the social unconscious

Class structure, gender roles, and the power structure of society are part of its foundation matrix. Dalal (1998, p. x) writes that the social unconscious "... is a representation of the institutionalisation of social power relations in the structure of the psyche itself". Later (2001), he examines the consequences of these social power relations for the contents of the social unconscious: "the social unconscious ... includes the power relationships *between* discourses" (p. 212). Brown (2001) describes four ways in which the social unconscious is manifested, among them being structural oppression—control of power and information by competing interests in society and the international community.

The question of power differences between men and women is an important aspect of the foundation matrix. There are social structures the unconscious aim of which is to maintain the power array between the genders. In traditional/conservative societies (for example, in all Muslim countries mentioned above), the purpose of blatant gender discrimination is to guarantee that men keep their power over women. These social mechanisms are unnoticeable to the naked eye, but are available to deeper analysis.

Paying attention to the ways in which fairy tales (especially *Cinderella*, which is so popular) reflect (and shape) gender relations and power structure in society could contribute an important perspective to the understanding of hidden social structure and norms and conventions. Fairy tales present female role models that are too dependent on men (Bacchilega, 1997; Butler, 1990; Warner, 1994). In contrast to the male heroic figures in genres such as legends or myths, heroines such as Cinderella and Snow White are not heroic figures. The European Cinderella usually passively waits for her Prince Charming to find her, which reflects how women followed this model for centuries. Stereotypical representations of the female role as passive and dependent in the very popular Cinderella story, as well as popular cultural products such as the Disney film, strongly shape our psyche. The unconscious symbolic meaning of the shoe, mentioned before, as entrapping the woman's body (foot), signifies the possession of women and their bodies by men. The fact that this motif repeats itself even in societies where the shoe and the foot are considered dirty and inferior illustrates well the deep social assumption that women belong to their male relatives (husbands, brothers, fathers) who hold the power in their relationship.

As noted above, the idea of the shoe fitting the foot might also evoke a feeling of being enveloped, contained, and protected. However, it hides the idea that women are weak, needing strong men to protect them. It actually signifies benevolent sexism, which is a chivalrous attitude toward women that feels favorable but is actually sexist because it casts women as weak creatures in need of men's protection.

In certain cultures, the name of the heroine in Cinderella also tells us about the deep unconscious attitude towards women in that society. The name Cinderella comes from cinders, ashes, or, to be precise, partly burned coal or wood that has stopped giving off flames. In English, the meaning of the name Cinderella is "little cinder girl". In French, the meaning of the name Cinderella is "of the ashes". In Portuguese, the story is known as *Gata Borralheira* (Cinder Kitty) and she was described as "covered in ash". In Hebrew, she was called "the dirty one" (*Lichluchit*). Such a pejorative name actually demonstrates a hidden identification with the mean stepmother and her daughters.

Various scholars point out that the shoe is an erotic object, symbolizing sexual relations and marriage consummation. Cox (1893) mentions that certain ethnic groups celebrated betrothal by putting on a shoe, and that in central Europe it was common to throw a shoe at newlyweds to ensure a successful sex life. Dundes (1987b, p. 60) reminds us that the sexual symbolism of shoes is well documented and survived in modern folklore as the custom of placing shoes on the rear bumpers of cars carrying newlyweds off to their honeymoons, or in nursery rhymes in which old women who live in shoes have lots of children. In Judaism, the shoe is also linked with sex. Nacht (1915) argues that the shoe symbolizes women and that this explains the ritual of the Halitzah in the Jewish tradition (the removal of the sandal of the wife's brother-in-law when her husband dies). He also points out that the shoe is further connected to relations between the sexes in that it symbolizes authority (pp. 166–67).

Having this in mind, it is possible to view the realization of the idiom "no one can fit into her shoe", appearing in this fairy tale, as reviving sensations and emotions associated with feelings of owning and possessiveness. A certain foot, surrounded and enveloped by a unique shoe, demonstrates the exclusiveness within couples. However, only the woman is being possessed and the shoe motif always appears in the context of womanhood, in all societies around the world in which this fairy tale is told. Being enveloped by a shoe might evoke the sensation of being embraced, contained, and, therefore, beloved. However, it could also potentially evoke the sense of being trapped, captured, and imprisoned. Muhawi's interpretation of the centrality of the woman's body in the Cinderella tale (focusing on tale type AT510B, in which the daughter has to marry her father) is in line with this view. In the versions in which the daughter obtains a disguise that covers her body, Muhawi views the disguise in which the daughter escapes as a mask that appears to change the identity of the heroine, altering how others, especially men, perceive her body. The mask/disguise covering the heroine's body is not finally removed until the discovery of her true identity, which in many versions is enabled by the shoe, and the fact that "no one can fit into the heroine's shoe". Whereas the disguise camouflages her feminine identity, the shoe reveals it.

Another social aspect revealed through the idiomatic expression "no one fits into her shoe", concretely portrayed in these fairy tales, is the romantic idea that there is only one woman that suits her prince. Romantic love, which is so highly praised in literature and films, was not always the main reason for marriage. Actually, it is only in recent generations that people marry out of love. Before the twelfth century, in Europe, love between men and women was not regarded as heroic; it was instead considered a sign of weakness, the preoccupation of a person without character.[22] Romantic love generally involves a mix of emotional and sexual desire: emotional highs, exhilaration, passion, and elation. Romantic love is passionate, but the passion itself is not the only feature of this type of love. Hidden in it is the idea of marital monogamy, so important to society through the centuries, as it guarantees stability of social institutions such as the family, and the provision of protective conditions for growing children. These fairy tales serve as a hidden social agent that both reflects the idea that "there is only one foot that fits one shoe", meaning that only one specific woman is suitable for a particular man, but also enhances and crystallizes it.

The popular American comedy-drama film, *In Her Shoes* (2005, directed by Curtis Hanson with an adapted screenplay by Susannah Grant and starring Cameron Diaz, Toni Collette, and Shirley MacLaine), presents the double function of shoes in human experience. Based on the novel of the same name by Jennifer Weiner, the film might serve as a good example of the way in which shoes are perceived in women's world. The film focuses on the relationship between two sisters and their grandmother. In accordance with our perspective here, the shoes carry both concrete and symbolic meanings. On the concrete level, the eldest sister (Rose, an ostensibly plain and serious lawyer who is protective of Maggie despite her flaws) uses numerous pairs of shoes in order to feel good about herself, as she is not satisfied with the way she looks (which is even more difficult when she compares herself to her beautiful sister, Maggie). Maggie is a free spirit who is unable to hold a steady job (due to her virtual inability to read) and turns to alcohol and men for emotional and financial support. The sisters share nothing in common but their shoe size. On the abstract level, the film describes the gradual process in which each sister learns how to put herself in her sister's shoes and learn something about "the other".

In summary, the Cinderella versions, although they vary in many ways, all contain the idea that only one woman's foot fits into a specific shoe, thus concretely demonstrating the idiomatic expression: "no one can fit into her shoe". This fairy tale reflects and constructs the social norm that women are possessed by men, and the exclusivity of marriage.

CHAPTER SEVEN

Fire of lust: passion and greed in fairy tales and the social (un)conscious

> "Can a man take fire in his bosom, and his clothes not be burned?"
>
> (Proverbs 6:27,28)

The scene of molten lava flowing, burning everything on its way, is always fascinating. Everything in the path of an advancing lava flow will be knocked over, ignited by the extremely hot temperature. When lava enters a body of water, it can boil violently and cause an explosive shower of molten spatter. The most breathtaking and mesmerizing experience is when it enters the ocean. The sea churns as molten hot lava oozes across the ground or into the ocean. The attraction of those scenes stems from the seemingly uncontrollable power of nature, perhaps reflecting similar forces inside our souls, and our dynamic struggle to control them.

The above description demonstrates the intense force of fire and the fact that it can be both a source of power and life energy and, at the same time, a source of destruction and devastation. In order to channel this force towards life and not death, we should manage fire well, developing the knowledge of how to deal with powerful energy sources. It is not surprising that this quality of fire serves in our language to describe intense feelings such as love, passion, envy, and greed. Similar to fire, love and passion can be benevolent if handled appropriately. Just as with fire, they are not only beneficial, but essential to maintain psychic liveliness. However, when uncontrolled, they have the potential to burn everything around. This is the subject of this chapter, examining the realization of an idiomatic expression that includes the word fire as appearing in a fairy tale that deals with greed. In this way, the pictorial–sensorial realm meets the metaphoric one.

The idiomatic expression "fire of lust" is concretely portrayed in the fairy tale below, recorded in the IFA.

The poor brother, the eagle, and the treasure

In one of the villages of the Punjab district in India, there lived two peasant brothers. One of them succeeded in everything: His rice's fields were bountiful, his granary always full of rice. The second brother was poor. His meagre rice crop was not enough to feed his family. Sometimes, he had no seeds for the coming planting season. One year there was a drought. When all the peasants started to work their land, he did the same, as he hoped to beg a few seeds from his neighbors and return them after the harvest. But, when he asked his neighbor for seeds, he refused. He went to a second neighbor who also refused and blamed him for not asking his rich brother. Sad and disappointed, he went to his brother, who lived in a splendid palace. As the gate was locked, he knocked until his brother's wife shouted at him. He asked her for a little rice and told her that he was afraid of missing the planting season. She replied angrily, "We know you are an unsuccessful person. Could you not have saved a little rice"?

He wished to say something, but could not find the right words. She brought him some cooked rice from the kitchen, put it in a sack and gave it to him. He did not believe it could be used to plant the new crop. Only after he had returned home and went to put the sack on the carriage, did he realize that the rice was cooked. He wanted to kill himself, but he pitied his wife and children and was ashamed to tell them what had happened. He decided to plant the rice, and leave the rest to fate. The rice did not grow and the poor brother was deeply distraught. One day, when he went to the field as usual, he saw a strange plant growing. He did not know what it was, but his heart told him to care for it. When the harvest approached, he took a scythe and went to the field, thinking to cut down the big plant. At that moment, a large eagle came down from the sky, took hold of the plant and tried to fly away with it, but the poor brother grasped the plant strongly in both hands. The eagle carried him up into the sky. After a few hours, the eagle began his descent, until he stood on a hill on which gold bullion and amethysts were scattered. The poor brother stood up and did not know what to do. The eagle told him: "Take whatever you wish from this treasure and fill your pockets, but remember: In one hour, we must leave this place; otherwise, we are lost—a fire will break out on the hill and destroy everything."

"I ... am ready to leave at this ... moment", the poor brother stuttered. "I have already taken one piece of gold bullion and one amethyst and I am satisfied with this".

The eagle was surprised and replied, "That is well, if you are satisfied with this, your good future is promised. Let us depart."

The poor brother grasped the plant and the eagle flew and brought him back to his field. He cut a piece of the gold bullion and went to sell it to the goldsmith. He had enough money to buy food and clothes for himself and his family. He did this whenever he needed to and still had enough gold left over. He soon started buying new land lots, and planting them; he soon became the richest man in his village. His sister-in-law regretted her past behavior and could not understand how her poor brother-in-law had become so rich. She asked her husband to invite his brother. At first, he hesitated, but then decided that he had to be as greedy as his brother ...

He invited his brother and was especially kind to him. Then he asked him how he had attained his riches. His brother agreed to tell him, even though the rich brother had refused to help him when he was poor. He told his brother that he had wanted to kill himself out of despair, but did not do so because of his wife and children. He explained how he had planted the cooked rice given to him by the rich brother's wife. He told him about the plant that had grown out of the rice and the way he had cared for it, up until the eagle arrived, kidnapped him, and brought him to the hill with the treasure. He told him that he took only one piece of gold bullion and one amethyst.

"Wonderful!" said the rich brother, and planned how he would become even richer than his brother, because his brother knew nothing about amethysts. He planted one plot with cooked rice and went every day to see if the plant had grown. One day he was happy to see such a plant growing; he began to nurture it with great care. When harvest approached, he went to the field to harvest to plant. All of a sudden, an eagle came down and tried to take the plant, but the rich brother was ready. He grasped the plant with both hands. The eagle asked, "Why are you holding my plant?" The rich brother replied, "I want you to bring me to the hill with the treasure."

"Are you poor, too?" asked the eagle. "Yes", lied the rich brother.

"Well, then, I will bring you there", said the eagle, and flew away. They reached the hill with the gold and amethysts. The eagle warned the rich brother that after one hour a fire would burst out and destroy everything.

The rich brother agreed not to take too much gold and amethysts, but in his heart of hearts he thought differently. He started looking for bigger and more precious stones and did not notice that time was passing. The eagle tried to warn him, but the rich brother said, "One moment; I will just fill my hat and my pockets." The eagle waited until the last moment; when he saw that the rich brother still hadn't returned, he flew away from the hill. When the brother felt the heat coming up from the earth, he knew he was in danger. He ran to look for the eagle, but the eagle was no longer there. The rich brother was burned in the fire of his lust, his pockets full of gold and precious stones.

This tale was recorded in the IFA by Moshe Haimowits in the year 1976. He heard it from Yitzhak Sasson, who was born and raised in Bombay. Typologically, it may be qualified as a Jewish Oicotype AT*676a, named "Two Brothers—Rich and Poor".

Following in the wonder-tale tradition, this tale is full of magical transformations and objects, providing it with a fantastic nature. The fantastic quality contributes to the feeling of being detached from reality, and enhances an experience relating to the primary levels of consciousness. A close examination of the magical objects and transformations in the tale reveals the immediate connection and the total correspondence between the concrete form of some of the marvellous elements and the mental ideas dealt with in the tale, as well as the tale's messages.

The central message of the tale is quite clear, preaching modesty and abstemiousness. This message is overtly presented in the eagle's words when he hears the poor brother say he has taken only one piece of gold bullion and only one amethyst: "If you are modest, your good future is promised". Unlike the poor brother, the rich brother is greedy. As he was not satisfied with only one piece of gold bullion and one amethyst, he remained on the mountaintop filling his pockets, until he was burned in the fire. This action, in which the rich brother's greediness and unrestrained lust for gold causes him to be burnt in the fire, may be viewed as a realization of a very familiar idiomatic expression existing in many different languages: "fire of lust". As will be presented later, this idiom appears in the various spoken languages of the Jewish communities that preserve and tell this tale. The verbal–metaphoric level and the actual–concrete level become united in our version in a way that intensifies both levels. Both modes of thought processes (primary and secondary, in Freudian terminology) present precisely the same idea, using two different modes of expression: the concrete and the abstract. The concrete manner in which the greedy brother is punished visually demonstrates the way in which his greediness causes him to be burnt in the fire. This clearly reflects the metaphorical meaning of the idiomatic expression: "fire of lust", as well as the central message of the tale, which is also told overtly in the text.

Cross-cutural aspects—burnt in the fire of lust: managing desire

The idiomatic expression "fire of lust" describes a person whose lust knows no bounds, until it destroys him/her. Greed and lust are mentioned among the seven deadly sins, fundamental to Catholic confessional practices. "You shall not covet" is also one of the Ten Commandments. It is an imperative against setting one's desire on things that are forbidden, and avoiding greed for things we might long for. Clearly, if lust and greed were not essential parts of human nature, there would be no need for such a commandment.

Lust, like love and passion, is one of those traits that need to be handled properly, in order to ensure joy and prevent disaster. Interestingly enough, in another story about India, the well known *Jungle Book* by Rudyard Kipling, Bagheera suggests that Mowgli brings "the Red Flower" (meaning fire) that men grow in their village to have a strong friend against Shere Khan, Mowgli's enemy. That story focuses on the ability of men to control fire and use its power for protection.

Two Iraqi parallels of this type are recorded in the IFA. In the language spoken by the Jews of Iraq, it is common to say: "*K'albu Michruk*", which means that the person's heart is burnt when s/he lusts for or desires something. There are several similar idioms in this language, such as: "*Kishtail K'albu*" (the heart is excited, inflamed, it burns out of love), "*K'albu Nar*" (the heart is a fire), and "*Nar Shukuhu*" (fire of lust). The fire in these expressions is perceived as having two meanings: the fire that revives (rebirth) and the fire that destroys. Proverbs and sayings of Iraqis explain the way in which fire is associated, on the one hand, with positive qualities such as love and passion (as in the expression "*Mashul Bnaru*", which means inflamed by fire, or in love), but also with negative feelings and emotions, such as anger. The Iraqi proverb "*Inaf Nar v Inaf Ditan*" (one nostril produces fire, and the other, smoke) exemplifies the negative quality of fire, as it describes an extremely angry person. The multitude and plurality of idioms and proverbs relating to fire, and the way in which fire is associated with love, lust, greediness, and anger, might touch upon the central place of both perceptions of fire in human (un)consciousness. In a Jewish–Iraqi folk-song, a line is: "*Lola Lahiv il Nar Bechloi Adomak*": "If not for the fire's flames [of my heart], I would have embraced you". In this case, as in the others exemplified here, fire is associated simultaneously with love and danger. If it were not for the fire that burns, the beloved could enjoy and fulfill his love. However, when the fire is too strong, and when something which is basically good becomes extreme, the result can be destructive. There is an example of the same idea that appears in another Jewish–Iraqi folk-song: "*Shift il Tsava min Baid Gilt Achtragna*": "I saw the light [of the lover], I thought we were burned up".

Basically, wilfulness, passion, and lust are positive qualities, related to life and essential to the preservation of life on the individual level, as well as the continuity of the species. However, when they deviate from an appropriate measure, problems might ensue. It is no accident that fire is chosen to represent these qualities, as it, too, carries the same ambivalent nature; in order for fire to nurture life, it must be managed properly. The historical event in which mankind learned how to produce fire is crucial in the history of humanity. The myth about Prometheus (see later) is one of the famous expressions of the way in which fire is perceived by mankind, and its centrality in culture. Nevertheless, in the same way that fire is essential for life (fire plays a key role in numerous important endeavours, such as cooking and the production of energy, light, warmth, and so forth), an inappropriate use of fire leads to burning, destruction, and annihilation—all of which violates the very value of life. Indeed, this is exactly the idea expressed in the tale about the poor and the rich brothers. More than anything else, the story emphasizes the importance of knowing the proper measure. Excess is recognized in the tale with a concrete fire, which burns and destroys the rich, greedy brother. In the tale, the "fire of lust" attains a concrete translation, when real flames burn the brother who did not know where to stop. The concluding sentence in the tale: "The rich brother was burned in the fire of his lust, his pockets full of gold and precious stones" provides a clear demonstration of the link between fire and lust.

It is important to note that the tale does not reduce the importance of will, wishing, and desire. On the contrary: It emphasizes the will of the poor brother, who never gave up, even in his most difficult moments. We might say that, in spite of his despair, he was flamed by the fire of life. This is a fire that encourages humans to live and function in a useful way. The rich brother's lust, however, does not operate as a reviving force, but, rather, as a source of annihilation. The opposing ways in which the brothers are related to each other can be seen as a mediating form of the binary opposition, life–death, to speak in the terms of Lévi-Strauss, fire being one of its agents.

The fire on the mountain is seemingly external to the rich brother. The wonder-tale, whose plot progresses through action, finds a picturesque way to describe fire, which might be arbitrary, and receives no logical explanation. The plot does not clarify why a fire should burn someone who does not leave the mountain in time. Like many other issues, this point remains unclear and somewhat detached. A person who burns in a fire with his pockets full of treasures might visually demonstrate the main idea embedded in the idiomatic expression "fire of lust".

Fire, myths, and human development

The tale reminds us that we, as human beings, should learn to manage our desire and avoid the poles and extremes of emotions and behaviors. However, doing it through the concreteness of fire addresses archaic modes of mental organization, when the baby's inner world is still filled with instinctual experiences, imagining its satisfaction through devouring the breast. This mode is fundamental to all human beings as part of their early development. Actually, one of the features distinguishing an adult from an infant is the amount of control attained over impulses and drives. A mature adult has learned to delay gratification and not succumb to lust, in contrast to a child. When a child gradually acquires a certain measure of self-mastery, a way of regulating his/her own impressions and impulses, this can be regarded as a civilizing process (Elias, 1994) at the individual level.

Human ontogenesis recapitulates phylogenesis, and we can easily track the development of mankind and civilization as following the same line. The ability to make and control fire—which is necessary for cooking, making pottery and glass, and metalworking—sets people apart from the animals. Eriksen (2007) mentions that fire management strategies were a source of conflict between indigenous people and Western cultures, whether in Australia or the USA. Indigenous use of fire, whether for resource harvesting, hunting, vegetation and soil generation, or maintenance of communal areas, were seen as an evil, environmentally degrading practice, as such fires threatened both the properties and social hierarchy of rigidly ordered colonial societies. It seems as if colonial societies perceived themselves as more "developed" and the indigenous people as "primitive", thus failing to see the fire knowledge of local people as a result of their historical experience, borrowing the concept of "proper training" from child-rearing practices to apply it to fire management.

Gautam (1990) states that Hinduism recognizes fire as one of the five basic elemental matters which constitute the entire universe: earth, water, fire, air, and space. The presence of fire is necessary for all five pious occasions being celebrated in the entire life of a Hindu. Agni is one of the most important of the Hindu–Vedic gods. He is the god of fire and the acceptor of sacrifices. He is ever young, because the fire is relit every day, yet he is also immortal.

Islanders of the Pacific Ocean have a myth in which a snake asks his human children to cook some fish. The children simply heat the fish in the sun and eat it raw, so the snake gives them fire and teaches them to use it to cook their food. It is worth noting that whereas in the Bible story of the Garden of Eden, the snake brings knowledge by tempting Eve to eat the apple, in the above myth, it brings knowledge by granting fire. In both cases the snake is associated with bringing knowledge that is a crucial event in the history of humanity. Another example of the same idea is portrayed in the Greek myth of Prometheus, equating fire with the dawn of human intellect, enlightenment, and power. This ancient myth tells us that when the god Zeus decided to create mortal man, he told Prometheus to endow him with all the good virtues and gifts of the gods except fire. Fire was exclusively reserved for the use of the gods. However, Prometheus came to the conclusion that the presence of fire is extremely necessary for mankind, so he decided to steal fire from the heavens. When Zeus discovered this, he designed a "wild fire" which would ruin human civilization whenever humanity crosses the boundary of sins. We can easily see the reflection of this myth in the above fairy tale.

The mythology of ancient Egypt contains a large, magnificently colored bird named the Phoenix. According to the myth, the Phoenix lived for up to 600 years. At the end of its life, the great creature built a funeral pyre (fire) and immolated (sacrificed) itself. From the funeral fire's ashes, a new Phoenix emerged with the freshness of youth to live out yet another cycle of life, death, and rebirth. Perhaps, in this myth, we can see the dual role of fire as both destroying and annihilating life and also as reviving and energizing life (retrieved from US national park service: www.nps.gov/fire/wildland-fire/learning-center/fire-in-depth/cultural-interp-fire.cfm)

Other myths from ancient Italy tell of the guardian priest, the King of the Wood. He was regarded as the spirit of vegetation and was believed to be endowed with the magical power to make trees bear fruit. While his life was held precious by his worshipers, the very value attached to it ensured his death. The ritual killing of the incarnate Tree Spirit was believed to be the only way of preserving the spirit from inevitable decay. Each King of the Wood had to be burnt by fire so that the divine Tree Spirit within him would be transferred in its entirety to a younger and more robust successor (Frazer, 1922).

Inspired by Elias's book, *The Civilizing Process* (1994), where Elias studied changes in manners, society, and personality in Western Europe, Goudsblom, in his book, *Fire and Civilization* (1992), argues that the control of fire, even before the development of speech or the making of tools, differentiated human beings from all their ancestors. He assesses the significance of fire in culture, suggesting that dread of hell-fire developed as people learned to fear fire in war and in cities.

However, humans could turn the destructive force of fire into productive use, and, thus, give it a purpose. He claims that there is a level at which a civilizing process can be discerned: The level of human history at large. Goudsblom states that "the control of fire is an integral aspect of human life, undeniably involving foresight and renunciation of primary impulses" (p. 3), thus it resides in our social unconscious.

The control of fire was always social: it could only be sustained by a group. The fairy tale, as a social product, reveals, in its unique language, the intricate interplay between both constructive and destructive aspects of human energy and desire. The fire is presented in its destructive quality as far as (wo)man cannot control and master his/her desire. In this way, we can see the parallel between content and form: Whereas the ability to control fire is associated with the shift from savage life to civilization (a critical turning point in human history), so does the fairy tale genre portray the borderline between two modes of human experience—concrete and abstract. When it tells of a man who is burnt in the fire of lust, using pictorial and verbal expressions as well, both modes are combined in a way that echoes primary experiences in human life and its connection to more developed ones.

Fire rituals

Myths, rituals, and fairy tales are part of the social unconscious (Weinberg, 2007). However, there are some differences between those social products: Whereas myths reflect the thinking of the people in the ancient world, where the connections between man and gods, fantasy and reality, one entity and another were less differentiated, rituals and ceremonies became more structured and organized social behaviors and fairy tales represent a more developed literature genre compared to myths. As said in the introduction to this book, fairy tales retain traces of an earlier evolutionary stage, when our forefathers had not yet advanced very far down the path towards higher individual development (Steiner, 1911). Tylor (1958) viewed folktales as examples of survivals from earlier cultural stages that could be interpreted to reveal earlier stages in human thought processes. Although all these social manifestations belong to the foundation matrix, just as fairy tales developed later than myths, rituals and ceremonies are also more elaborated social products usually transforming myths into public activities organized by priests or other leaders.

Fire ceremonies are the centre of many spiritual practices and common among all ancient and native cultures. A fire ceremony is considered the most powerfully transformative of all rituals, probably due to its purifying quality. Many cultures have myths and rituals involving fire and some religions worship fire. The term "fire-worshippers" is primarily associated with Zoroastrians. Fire rituals are often based on myths and legends about fire or fire gods. In ancient Rome, a sacred flame associated with the goddess Vesta represented national wellbeing. Women called the Vestal Virgins had the holy duty of keeping that flame alive (Staples, 1998). The Aztecs of ancient Mexico believed that the fire god Huehueteotl kept earth and heaven in place. At the end of each cycle of fifty-two years, they extinguished all fires, and Huehueteotl's priests lit a new flame for the people to use (Nicholson, 1971). In northern Europe, which has long, dark, cold winters, fire was especially honored. Pagan fire festivals such as lighting bonfires on May 1 have continued into modern times in European communities. We can see how fire rituals played an essential role in the foundation matrices of many cultures and societies.

Specific social aspects—back to fairy tales

Keeping in mind that the above fairy tale was told in a Jewish community, there might be an association to a legend about Moses as an infant being tested by the Egyptian Pharaoh after Moses had put Pharaoh's crown on his head, offering him a plate of hot coals as an alternative to a plate of gold. Moses started to grab for the gold. However, an angel intervened, shoved the gold to the side, and Moses not only grabbed the hot coal, but then put the coal into his mouth. As a result, he became "slow of speech and slow of tongue" (See Exodus 4:10). This is a story with a clear moral about the dangers of impulsivity and greed. We can add that much later in the story of Moses the demand of the Israelis in the desert from Aaron, Moses' brother to create a concrete God, led to the golden calf, for which they were severely punished by God. Here we have another connection between gold, impulsivity, and sibling rivalry, especially as our fairy tale is about brothers, the rich and the poor. This theme also pertains to rivalry among a variety of sub-groups, and is, therefore, relevant at the societal level.

In addition, we should remember the fate of Korach and 250 chieftains of the Israelite community who rose up against the leadership of Moses and Aaron (Numbers 16:1–18:32). God caused the earth to swallow up Korach and his people, and a fire consumed the 250 chieftains. Interestingly enough, one of the meanings of Korach's names is ICE. The fairy tale certainly reminds us of this story.

Later, when the Israelis entered their Promised Land, they had to fight the local tribes inhabiting Canaan. The Book of Joshua (Chapter 7) contains a narrative in which Achan incurred the wrath of God by coveting prohibited gold and silver that he found in the destruction of Jericho. Having been identified, his punishment was to be stoned to death. Apparently, the sin of greed and covetousness is seriously punished by God. We can imagine the intensity of these forces, as only severe punishment might eliminate them.

Summary

Learning to control fire is a form of civilization. Because humans tamed fire and incorporated it into their own societies, the societies became more complex and the people themselves became more civilized. The same process occurs in the ontogenetic and phylogenic level. Children also need to learn to master their impulses and delay gratification. The fairy tale about the two brothers reflects those civilization processes in both individual and social level, and the idiomatic expression "fire of lust", realized in the plot, beautifully reflects the nature of uncontrollable fire and its parallel inner processes of greed and lust. The idiomatic expression, as an intersection at which both verbal and somatic dimensions meet, is an important key to deciphering, understanding, and interpreting the marvellous nature that characterizes this fairy tale, and the social unconscious.

CHAPTER EIGHT

"To eat a crow" (swallow frogs): a story of decrees and humiliation

"If it's your job to eat a frog, it's best to do it first thing in the morning. And if it's your job to eat two frogs, it's best to eat the biggest one first"

(Mark Twain, accessed at: http://izquotes.com/quote/187974)

T he following example demonstrates how the familiarity with an idiomatic expression that exists in the spoken language of a certain society helps to shed light on the magical events appearing in the tales told by this society. This example can be classified as a version of the well known and widespread fairy tale, *Snow White*. Sixteen variants of *Snow White* are recorded in the Israeli Folktale Archie (IFA); most of them originated from Islamic countries (one from Tunis, six from Yemen, one from Persia, one from Egypt, one from Libya, one from Israeli Druze, two from Morocco, and two Muslim Palestine versions). Many of them include only single elements of the Snow White tale, usually the opening scene in which the envious stepmother wishes to get rid of her beautiful stepdaughter.

Three of these oral fairy tales, told by three different tellers (two from Morocco and one from Yemen) present a heroine who is forced to swallow frogs, or similar creatures. We suggest viewing this apparently bizarre plot detail as a realization of the idiom which exists in various forms in the languages spoken by this society, such as "to eat crow" or "to swallow a frog/snake".

One Moroccan version of *Snow White* recorded in the IFA is called "The orphan girl and the evil stepmother" (IFA 6766). This tale was recorded in the year 1965 and is reproduced below.

The orphan girl and the evil stepmother: a Moroccan version of Snow White

A woman died right after giving birth to a baby girl. The father remarried another woman who had seven daughters. The orphan became very beautiful. The stepmother envied her beauty and wished to humiliate her in front of her father. She forced her to drink water with seven small frogs in it so that the frogs would grow in her belly and her belly blow up. Then she told the father that his daughter was pregnant. She ordered him to kill her. He took the daughter to a far mountain and left her alone. After three days a man with a donkey, who was taking salt to the city, passed by. She ate some salt and vomited the frogs. She walked for three days until she found a hut belonging to seven brothers. When they went out to work, she cleaned their hut and prepared food. Then she hid in the storeroom. The brothers tried to figure out the mystery: Who did all this? Each night one brother was charged to watch and not fall asleep, but they failed. When the youngest brother was in charge, he cut his finger so it bled and he couldn't sleep and so found her. They got married and had a son. She went to visit her father and told him everything and he burnt his wife to death.

We can see that even though it is easy to notice the similarities between this version and the international Snow White type, some characteristics have been changed according to the social context in which it is told. For example, in South Africa, portraying the heroine figure as "white as snow" (motif Z65.1, appearing in the European versions) is not reasonable. Indeed, this characteristic is absent in the Moroccan version.

However, a major change, which is of special interest, appears in the opening of the tale, in which a maiden is forced by her evil stepmother to swallow a frog, so that her belly blows up, exposing her to slander for becoming pregnant out of wedlock. In this way, the stepmother hopes to get rid of the daughter, since her father will not accept this kind of promiscuity. The evil stepmother (motif S31 in the Arne–Thompson motifs classification index) who wishes to get rid of an extremely beautiful daughter (Motif M312.4) is identical to the international tale type. However, the Jewish–Moroccan version presents a unique form of this act, in which an idiomatic expression is hidden behind the concrete plot. The stepmother orders the maiden to swallow seven frogs. In the society in which this story is told, having sex out of wedlock is taboo and a maiden who does not obey this taboo is condemned to social isolation and is in danger of being banished.

In other Moroccan versions of this tale, the heroine is forced to swallow snakes. Both idioms—to swallow frogs and to swallow snakes, meaning to be forced to do something unpleasant and humiliating—exist in Murgab and French languages spoken by Moroccan Jews. A certain form of this idiom exists also in Mugrab: *bleh (ayin) zrana*. It is also possible that the Moroccan Jews knew this idiom in its French version: *avalé des couleuvres*, which means to accept something against your will, to live with it and get over it. Deciphering this idiom helps us understand the strange decree given by the stepmother. It is possible that the Jews in Morocco knew this idiom from various sources. Fruchtman and colleagues (2001, p. 52) attribute the origin of this idiom to French. They assume that this idiom originated from a story about a man who had to choose one punishment out of three: beating, swallowing frogs, and banishment. Eventually, he suffered all three.

It is worthwhile to note that here, too, the idiom "to burn with jealousy" becomes realized, while the jealous stepmother is literally burned (motif Q414.4 in the Aarne–Thompson classification index).

Deciphering the phenomenon of the realization of the idiom "to swallow the frog" enables us to see both levels of thought processes. The heroine, indeed, has to "swallow the frog" ("to eat a crow") in both abstract and concrete manner: she not only has to cope with a difficult life situation that is brought upon her against her will, she also literally swallows a frog. This is a maiden whose ability to independently manage her life and take control over it is quite limited. She lost her mother prematurely and found herself subjected to an evil stepmother who manipulated her father and influenced him against her. At the mercy of adults, she has to swallow any frog that is required. Indeed, other Jewish versions of this fairy tale emerging from Islamic countries present a heroine who is less helpless than the one portrayed in the famous European versions. The heroine in these versions is not "as white as snow", frozen, and lacking any vitality as is the Disney Snow White. Her name is associated with red and not with white (for example, in an Egyptian version her name is "Romana", which means in Arabic pomegranate, and her main characteristic is not necessarily beauty, but, rather, fertility). The red colour, in this case, is not associated with blood. Still, in all cases, including tales in which she takes initiative and is active, she has to cope with difficult injustices and tragic life circumstances. She also has to live with the fact of being neglected and persecuted by her stepmother. Truly, the decree to swallow the frog is always given by the evil stepmother, never by anyone else, in all versions of the tale. The father abandons her on the mountain, but the stepmother is the one who forced her to do things against her free will: to swallow the frogs.

Universal aspects

This apparently strange plot detail can be understood as a concrete translation of the idiomatic expression existing in Hebrew, as well as in other languages spoken by the communities in which the tale is common, "to swallow the frog" (*livloa et ha tzfardea*), which in American English appears as "to eat crow" or to be forced to accept a humiliating defeat. This expression, which is well known to the narrators and their audience, precisely conveys the existential situation of the maiden, who is forced to cope with the harsh demands of her evil stepmother. This tale-type is very common, and there are many different versions of it. Although some of its plot details are very strange and apparently bizarre, it still appears in many cultures, which raises the question of why it is so relevant to various people around the world. Perhaps this tale reflects and echoes themes that are relevant to the most primary, somatic levels of mental organization: the act of swallowing things is associated with deep emotions concerning what is allowed to enter the system and what is not welcome. Therefore, it is perceived as something that is "forced down the throat" by the external environment. The fairy tale genre, with its symbolic, abstract style, has found a subtle, sophisticated way of describing this situation, by hiding an idiomatic expression behind a concrete plot detail, combining abstract and concrete thought processes. On the personal level, the heroine is actually forced to "swallow the frog" ("to eat crow"). This is true on both the abstract and concrete levels: Parallel to the fact that, against her will, she must deal with horrific disasters, she actually swallows a frog. The fairy tale language, similar to dream language, conveys its messages by using visual, pictorial representations in order to describe an abstract mental situation.

Why was the frog chosen to demonstrate this idiomatic expression, related to an undesired and undesirable situation? In the Grimms' famous tale *The Frog King*, the frog is transformed into a handsome prince. In that tale, the heroine does not have to swallow a frog, but is forced to eat with the frog and sleep with the frog. In certain versions she also has to kiss it. In any case, the frog is associated with something that is forced upon her against her will. It is possible that the Grimm version presents a more delicate and sublimated form of the frog theme appearing in the Moroccan version. Jones (1951) interprets *The Frog King* tale as a story of a virgin overcoming her sexual fear. For Campbell (2008), an authority on mythology and a Jungian, the frog in the story symbolizes the unconscious, which at first sight is frightening but, when assimilated by the conscious ego, reveals itself for what it is—the total psyche, beautiful and true.

Perhaps choosing a frog has to do with its being a slimy, repulsive, sticky creature, in stark contrast to the charming prince. Another possibility is that this transformation hints at the physiological transformation the frog goes through during its lifecycle, from a tadpole to a mature frog, just as the girl in the tale changes from a young maiden into a married woman, and, in the Grimm version, the frog turns into a handsome groom.

Life begins in fresh water and then runs its course on dry land. Since water and earth are the living environments of frogs, the dual existence of the frog—both in water and on land—determines its double role in the Moroccan tale and other tales, situated as both an abstract linguistic expression and a concrete object that is actually swallowed. Both in life and in the tale, the frog represents the evolutionary process of many phyla that moved from their aqueous environment to a land environment, which also pertains to the caesura—from an intrauterine environment to a land environment.

We can find the symbol of the frog in many mythologies, playing the most significant role in Egyptian mythology: The frog-headed Heket is an Egyptian goddess of birth. In many cultures, the primary symbolic meaning of frogs deals with fertility. This is largely because these cultures observed frogs laying enormous quantities of eggs, therefore making it a fertility symbol as well as a symbol of abundance. Psychoanalytical interpretations of fairy tales, in which frogs and toads appear, associate tadpoles with sperm (Ribuoli & Robbiani, 1992).

Darwin described the somatic gestures of frogs as a response to external events. He explained the frogs' tendency to blow up as a survival attempt to frighten and a way to enlarge themselves and make it difficult for snakes to swallow them (Darwin, 1952, p. 105). The stepmother in the tale forces the heroine to swallow frogs, so that she blows up. Apparently, the fairy tale uses realistic characteristics (frogs' tendency to blow up) in order to provide the bizarre plot with "reasonable" explanations. Locating logical ways of thinking within a tale of magic creates a mixture combining both reality and fantasy in a way so typical of the fairy tale genre.

The thought processes presented in the tale express an encounter between two modes of experience and thought. The first is archaic, preverbal, and predominantly expressed through somatic sensations; the second is symbolic, represented by language. The early stage of human development, when human beings start out as embryos in the uterus (similar to the frog in water), is typified by a primary level of mental organization, lacking any symbolic capabilities. Similar to the prince in the Grimm version, who first turned into frog (before regaining his human shape) human beings also regressed from time to time to more archaic modes of expressions and the movement from one mode to another is bi-directional. Certain idiomatic expressions portrayed in the fairy tale link the two thought modalities, having both a concrete and an abstract pole, and reflect this bi-directional movement.

Specific social aspects

Dealing with the social unconscious, it is pertinent to ask what kinds of social desires, fears, traumas, and other social issues are reflected in the tale, and which societies preserve such tales. Based on a study that examined hundreds of fairy tales told by different ethnic communities in Israel, this tale type was found to be common among Jews who arrived in Israel from Islamic countries (Tunisia, Morocco, Yemen, Persia, Libya). The issue of having to accept an unwanted, humiliating attitude, forced upon one by a foreign government, is quite a familiar experience among these societies, which find it easy to identify with the heroine who "swallows frogs". From this perspective, swallowing the frog might express the existential situation of the Jewish community living in Morocco, governed by a foreign authority and being forced to accept harsh rules in order to survive. The heroine in the tale might represent the entire society, reflecting its morals, norms, and struggles. Scholars who have studied the life of the Jews in Morocco describe their difficulties during specific periods of time in Morocco (although not always), and the recurring theme of conflict and struggle in the folktales of Moroccan Jews (Noy, 1966; Saadon, 2004). Noy mentions that more than twenty Moroccan tales out of seventy-one preserved in the IFA deal with conflicts on the basis of national and religious issues.

Historically, after the Muslim conquest of Morocco in the seventh century, the rulers enforced a system of restrictions and decrees, the purpose of which was to grant privileges and respect to Muslims, and to humiliate other religions. Jews were forced to dress in clothes that identified them as different and to live in ghettos (*Malah*); they were forbidden to carry guns and forced to work at jobs considered inferior by the Arabs, among other restrictions. We cannot fully review here the life of the Jews in Morocco and this has been studied in other works (Bahloul, 1993; Levy, 2003; Saadon, 2004).

The meaning of "swallowing a frog" is understood as personal humiliation, and is universally relevant, regardless of background. However, this expression takes on a specific meaning in a particular social–historical context. The phenomenon of the stepmother parallels the phenomenon of the foreign regime. In each case, it is about a "parent" who is not the original or biological one. Whereas the foreign regime orders its "step-citizens" metaphorically or symbolically to "swallow frogs", the stepmother in the fairy tale forces her stepdaughter to swallow actual frogs. We should also bear in mind that a possible interpretation of swallowing a frog is that oral sex can be used as a contraceptive device, a way in which to refrain from having children, to suppress procreation. Control over sexual intercourse and conception is a universal phenomenon. This is especially important during times of military invasion, as is the raping of the subjugated women in order to create a sub-population with an ambiguous status. The transformations a frog goes through over the course of its life are also symbols of hope and development, which are extremely important to maintain in desperate times. Whereas this is always true, it seems to carry a special meaning for a society struggling with the difficulties of a foreign tyrant.

Another Jewish–Moroccan fairy tale preserved in the IFA, originating from Tanjir in the north part of Morocco, also presents the act of frog swallowing, which functions in exactly the same way. In both cases, it deals with a person who is forced to obey decrees that she cannot control. In this context, it is worth noting that the legal status of the Jews in Morocco was of what is called "protégé". This status, based on the Koran, gave them the privilege of living by their faith and religion. However, the governors had to humiliate them and collect a poll tax. Even if it is not necessary that the plot detail appearing in the Jewish–Moroccan *Snow White*, in which the heroine is forced to swallow frogs, is associated with these social facts, it is easy to see the parallelism between this detail and the humiliations brought upon the Jews in Morocco by the local government. This could be an example of the way in which a specific plot detail appears in the narrative for certain reasons which are more universal (such as the meaning of swallowing frogs as familiar to any human being, regardless of social and cultural context as the experience of being humiliated, which may be relevant to any one) but attains an additional meaning in a more specific historical and social context. Whereas the foreign governors metaphorically decreed the Jews to "swallow frogs", the evil stepmother does it literally and the heroine, with whom the storytelling society is identified, has to swallow actual frogs.

Of course, we should bear in mind that the attitude of the ruler towards the Jews was not always the same, and in certain eras Jews enjoyed better and more beneficial conditions. However, it was not in their power to control this and they were subjected to external influences, similar to the existential situation of the heroine in the Snow White tale. We can take as an example the time in which Morocco became France's protectorate, from the year 1912. Saadon (2004) mentions two interests involved in France's policy towards the

Jews: The need to strengthen their affinity to the country, create feelings of faithfulness among the Jews, avoid fomentation among them, and neutralize disagreements between the Jews and the local population. In addition, aiming to develop their economy, they tried to advance the Jewish population to a certain degree so they could gain benefit out of it. It is possible to say that the Jews had to "swallow many frogs" in order to survive under the foreign government. It is reasonable that stories about an abused, slandered stepdaughter who suffers humiliation and is banished from her home will be warmly embraced by a society living under these conditions.

This idea might be reinforced by the fact that this is not the only case in which a Jewish–Moroccan version of *Snow White* presents this bizarre plot detail, in which the heroine, with whom the society identifies, is forced to swallow frogs. In another Jewish–Moroccan tale preserved in the IFA, titled "Elijah the Prophet", a Rabbi and his wife died right after giving birth to a boy and a girl. The orphan twins became very close to each other. When they grew up, the sister chose a poor bride for her brother, as she thought she could make a good wife. However, the brother's wife envied the sister and forced her to swallow frogs. The brother thought that she was pregnant out of wedlock, and, following his wife's advice, took his sister to the forest and tried to kill her. Here, too, the concrete act of swallowing frogs is associated with the metaphorical meaning of the idiom "to swallow frogs". This tale was recorded in the IFA in the year 1963 and was told by a teller who arrived in Israel from Tangiers—a major city in northern Morocco with a large Jewish community. Due to its location on the Atlantic coast, it served as city of refuge for Jews during their expulsion from Spain. The Jews in Tangier were subjected to different rulers and treatment through the generations with little control over their conditions. We are not claiming that this is the reason for the appearance of the bizarre plot detail in the above fairy tale, in which the heroine is forced to swallow frogs. Rather, we suggest that a community which has to "swallow frogs" can easily adopt this kind of narrative and that we cannot ignore the parallels between the stepmother–stepdaughter relations in the story and that of the Moroccan Jews and the foreign government. This tale easily reflects and echoes issues with which the storytelling community is occupied.

EPILOGUE

In his provocative book, *A Brief History of Humankind* (2015), Harari suggests that what enabled Homo sapiens to become the most powerful and significant animal on the globe, jumping from being hunted by larger predators to the top of the food chain, is their ability to cooperate in large groups and to create societies. This achievement, he claims, would never have happened without the development of fictive language. By fictive language, he means that people were capable of using the language to discuss fiction, imaginary events, constructs, and ideas that do not exist in concrete reality, and agree about them. Fictive language allowed people not only to imagine things, but to imagine them *together*. This function enabled them to create religions, myths, organizations, and societies. Common myths, such as the Jewish ones on genesis and exodus, the myths of the Australian aborigine tribes on "dream time", or even national myths that each nation developed, would have never been created without this fictive language. People told one another stories, such as folktales and fairy tales, and through them they developed the wondrous abilities of collaboration and cooperation, which gave Homo sapiens a crucial advantage over any other creature, including other kinds of hominids. The important factor is that they all believed in those imagined myths and tales, and related to them as real and true. The hidden, unaware agreement to relate to fictive facts as if they are real actually stands as the basis of any collaboration of a group of people, whether they deal with business (and believe that a dollar has a specific value), work for a company (that is actually a legal entity that has nothing to do with the concrete materials or people who compose it), play together as a team (and believe in its fictitious goals), or feel their belonging to a specific nation (which is a fictive entity existing only in the mind of its citizens).

The social (un)conscious is built, among other factors, on the belief in those myths, folktales, and common assumptions, existing only in the joint imagination, or the minds, of people from the same society. Some of these beliefs are conscious, some are preconscious, and many are unconscious. Even when conscious, people might not be aware of the impact of those myths on their behavior. Any collaboration between members of a specific society is based on the same myths. Two Americans who have never met can collaborate and feel some belonging and connection because they both believe in the existence of the American nation, homeland, flag, and anthem, and its overt, tacit, and covert norms.

You might have noticed that we used the term social (un)conscious. In the process of writing this book, we hit upon a number of questions and dilemmas around the use of the social unconscious term. We noticed that some of the aspects discussed as part of the social unconscious are quite conscious. Indeed, in the introduction, we explained that "social unconsciousness" might not necessarily mean that the material is always unconscious, but, rather, that we are not necessarily aware of the ways and *extent* of its influence upon us. In addition, Hopper and Weinberg (2011) have already mentioned in their introduction to Volume I of their series of books about the social unconscious that it includes conscious, preconscious, non-conscious, and unconscious aspects. However, we were still uncomfortable with using a concept that includes the word "unconscious" when to some it is conscious, which seems contradictory. Our solution was to put (un) in parentheses and use the term social (un)conscious.

Fairy tales are part of the legacy of a certain society, and, as we claimed, it both shapes the national identity and reflects its deep and unconscious assumptions. For example, as described in the chapter about eyes and envy, the Grimm brothers' tales seem to influence and shape the German spirit (as mentioned, some claim that their cruelty is even responsible for the Nazis' atrocities) perhaps more than reflecting it. Fairy tales clearly represent this fictive language, as they describe imaginary events, unreal actions, and non-existing creatures, and it seems that the audience is ready to accept this fiction. However, the language of the fairy tales is more than fictive, as it hides some unexpected idiomatic expressions realized in the plot through the actions of the heroes. This hidden language has a powerful impact on the social unconscious (and also reflects some of its themes) because it resides on the border of concrete and symbolic language, thus having a liminal position.

In our book, we posited many examples of the realization of those idiomatic expressions, from several fairy tales, each chapter focusing on a certain expression and body part, showing its relevance to the social (un)conscious and to social issues, some of them relevant to the society in which those fairy tales were told, and some of them relevant to universal issues, hence belonging to the collective unconscious. Greed, envy, humiliation, possession, power struggles, gender issues, are all part of human nature and are common to many cultures; however, they can find different expressions in certain cultures.

Being group therapists and group analysts, which means believing that we cannot separate the individual from society and cannot talk about him or her outside their social context, we brought examples and vignettes from therapy groups to show how these issues portray themselves in the group matrix.

We hope that finishing this book opened the eyes (another idiomatic expression) of the readers to the hidden language of fairy tales, and brought them in touch with social issues that they were unaware of.

NOTES

1. Some of the ideas presented in this part also appear in Raufman (2012, 2015) and Raufman and Yigael (2010, 2011).
2. Aleph (A) is the first letter in the Hebrew alphabet.
3. Beth (B) is the second letter in the Hebrew Alpha-Bet.
4. The unconscious impact of words on the body is demonstrated in the following creative research (Bargh et al., 1996): Young students (age 18–22 years old) were requested to compose four word sentences from groups of five words (e.g., see, he, yellow, it, immediately). For one group of participants, half of the scrambled sentences included words associated with aging (e.g., Florida, forgetfulness, bald, grey or wrinkle). After the young people completed this task, they were requested to participate in another research in an office across the corridor. Their short walk to the office was the target of the experiment: The researchers secretly measured the time it took them to walk from one side of the corridor to the other side. The youngster who composed sentences related to aging walked significantly slower than the other students.
5. For example, Raufman and Yigael (in press) analysed the fairy tale "The Wolf and the Kids", and concluded that as the mother failed in protecting her kids, they were traumatized and had to develop a defense mechanism that includes escaping, hiding and evading.

6. In the Aarne Thompson index, this tale-type is classified as ATU 706.
7. Actually, Dundes has already raised the idea of viewing the father/brother who cuts off the maiden's hand as being associated with the idiom "to ask for her hand" (Dundes, 1987B, p. 61). However, he did not develop this idea in terms of the relations between different modes of experience.
8. This is a very intensive debate. Zipes, for example, highlighted the realities of child abuse, neglect, and abandonment in fairy tales, claiming that fairy tales, along with other folk narrative genres, express an adult perspective on power and the family (Zipes, 1995, p. 220). Tatar (1987, 1992) mentioned that viewing incest in fairy tales as the daughter's fantasy is part of the tendency to blame children's sexuality for what befalls them, "in part, out of a desire to avoid facing the 'unpleasant truths' that emerge once we concede that some of the events staged in fairy tale fictions can be as real as the fantasies they seem to represent" (Tatar, 1992, pp. xx–xxi).
9. In Basile's Penta of the Chopped-off Hands (2007), a long description is dedicated to the heroine's brother, who is fascinated by the loveliness of her hands. This description serves to explain the heroine's behavior; by cutting off her hands she loses her attractiveness in the eyes of her brother (see Schlauch, 1969). The chivalric romance La Manekine also provides another explanation for such behavior, since by law the king cannot marry a woman missing any part of her body (see Tatar, 1992).
10. In the collection *Druze Folktales*, published in 1978 (edited by Falah and Shenhar), Johara Ahchmed Hamza Azam is the only female teller among eight male tellers. In the collection *The Shadow of a Voice*, edited by Salman Falah (1983, first translated into Hebrew in 1977), all nine tales were told by male tellers.
11. In other languages (e.g., Hebrew) the idiom is "smooth as a baby's skin".
12. Even though this idiom does not appear exactly in the same way in English, it does appear in other languages. Anzieu related to the French idiom: *"faire peau neuve"* "to get inside the skin of a character", to turn over a new leaf (Anzieu, 1989, p. 13), to express issues of identification.
13. The protective function of the group skin-ego goes beyond the analytic endeavor, and is evident, for example, in studies about soldiers' PTSD following combat. Apparently, and contrary to common sense, the main factor that determines the prevalence of combat PTSD is the cohesion of the military unit (Brailey et al., 2007;

Browne et al., 2007). Soldiers' first motivation is not patriotic: they do not fight for their country. They fight for their friends-in-arms and for their military unit (Hughes et al., 2005). Belonging to the unit creates a group ego-skin, psychologically protecting them from the impact of stress. The social/national skin is there, but its protective function is weaker.

14. For example, some of the Grimms' fairy tales were influenced by Nordic mythology (e.g., "Sleeping Beauty" stems from the story of Brunhilde, in "The Ring Circle," exiled by her father Odin to the island of Iceland, protected by a ring of fire, awakened by Sigurd through rape).

15. We should bear in mind that nation-states evolved from the end of the eighteenth century onwards, with the idea that the state can treat large numbers of people equally by efficient application of the law through the bureaucratic machinery of the state. The rise of nation-states is associated with the rise of patriotic feelings at the beginning of the nineteenth century all over Europe. It received a philosophical underpinning in the era of Romanticism, at first as the "natural" expression of the individual peoples. Racism joined itself with colonialist imperialism and "continental imperialism", most notably in pan-Germanic and pan-Slavic movements. The relation between racism and ethnic nationalism reached its height in the twentieth century Fascism and Nazism.

16. Dégh suggests that "One glance at the Bolte-Polivka catalog or the Aarne-Thompson international tale typology shows that even the tales recorded from German informants are international" (p. 96).

17. Zipes mentions that it was a time of disillusionment, as the emancipation of the individual, eagerly sought by the Enlightenment writers, became fraught with difficulties by the end of the eighteenth century since it was no longer possible to assume that the individual could posit himself or herself in the world and become at one with it. Overcoming the alienating conditions for self-development and social emancipation could not be accomplished while the socio-political changes fostered conditions which led to reification of the individual: the production and use of human beings as if they were tools and commodities. Ironically, the Romantics had to attack the Enlightenment to try to enrich and fulfill its legacy of humanitarianism (1977, p. 423).

18. The power loss was preceded by a massive loss of population and of infrastructure (wealth) due to wars (in the seventeenth century, the Thirty Years War; during the sixteenth century, wars of reformation).

19. There are numerous articles and books relating to *Oedipus Rex* and to its psychoanalytic interpretations. For some that are more relevant to the theme of blindness and psychoanalytical thought, see Dodds (1973), Lacan (2007), Ziaul & Fahmida Kabir (2013).
20. We wish to thank Ezra Morad for this information.
21. We wish to thank Shoshana Molcho for this information.
22. In *The Allegory of Love* (1977), C. S. Lewis traces the invention of the narrative of romantic love—now the most standard of all loves recognized in the Western world. Romantic love is a Western invention, a near-obsession, supposedly the key to all happiness. For Lewis, the invention of romantic love in the age of the troubadours (the age of the Crusades) was far more momentous for the development of the West, and far more broadly influential than, say, the Protestant Reformation.

REFERENCES

Aarne, A., & Thompson, S. (1961). *The Types of the Folktale: A Classification and Bibliography*. Helsinki: Suomalainen Tiedeakatemia.

Alexander, T. (1994). "Hanninat Allah – A Judeo-Yemenite Version of Cinderella", *Pe'amim*, 53: 124–148 (Hebrew).

Allen, W. (1989). *New York Stories* (film). Buena Vista Pictures.

Anzieu, D. (1989). *The Skin-Ego*. New Haven, CT: Yale University Press.

Anzieu, D. (1999). The group ego-skin. *Group Analysis*, 32: 319–329.

Aristotle (1991). *The Metaphysics*, J. H. McMahon (Trans.). Amherst, NY: Prometheus Books.

Atashe, Z. (1995). *Druze and Jews in Israel. A Shared Destiny?* Brighton: Academic Press.

Bacchilega, C. (1993). An introduction to the "innocent persecuted heroine" fairy tale. *Western Folklore*, 52(1): 1–12.

Bacchilega, C. (1997). *Postmodern Fairy Tales: Gender and Narrative Strategies*. Philadelphia, PA: University of Pennsylvania Press.

Bahloul, J. (1993). Home and remembrance of the exile among North African Sephardim. *Jewish Folklore and Ethnology Review*, 15: 89–92.

Bargh, J. A., Chen, M., & Burrows, L. (1996). Automaticity of social behavior: direct effects of trait construct and stereotype activation on action. *Journal of Personality and Social Psychology*, 71: 230–244.

Bar-Itzhak, H. (1993). The Jewish Moroccan Cinderella in Israeli context. *Journal of Folklore Research*, 30(2–3): 93–125.

Basile, G. (1932). *The Pentamerone of Giambattista Basile*, N. M. Penzer (Ed.), B. Croce (Trans.). New York: Dutton.

Basile, G. (2007). Penta of the chopped-off hands. In: *The Tale of Tales* (pp. 223–231). Detroit, MI: Wayne State University Press.

Bauer, P. (2004). Getting explicit memory off the ground: steps toward construction of a neuro-developmental account of changes in the first two years of life. *Developmental Review, 24*: 347–373.

Ben-Amos, D. (1967). Narrative forms in the Magadha: structural analysis (unpublished PhD thesis). Bloomington, IN: Indiana University.

Ben-Amos, D. (1973). The 'myth' of Jewish humor. *Western Folklore, 32*: 112–131.

Ben-Dor, G. (1979). *The Druze in Israel. A Political Study, Political Innovation and Integration in a Middle Eastern Minority*. Jerusalem: Magnes Press.

Benedict, R. (1947). *The Chrysanthemum and the Sword: Patterns of Japanese Culture*. London: Secker & Warburg.

Benedict, R. (1949). Child rearing in certain European countries. *American Journal of Orthopsychiatry, 19*: 342–348.

Benjamin, J. (1988). *The Bonds of Love: Psychoanalysis, Feminism, and the Problem of Domination*. New York: Pantheon Books.

Berandt, C. (1968). *The Third Reich of Dreams*. Chicago, IL: Quadrangle Books.

Berman, A., Berger, M., & Gutmann, D. (2000). The division into Us and Them as a universal social structure. *Mind and Human Interaction, 11*(1): 53–72.

Bettelheim, B. (1976). *The Uses of Enchantment: The Meaning and Importance of Fairy Tales*. New York: Penguin.

Bick, E. (1968). The experience of the skin in early object relations. *International Journal of Psychoanalysis, 49*: 484–486.

Billow, R. M. (2003). *Relational Group Psychotherapy: From Basic Assumptions to Passion*. London: Jessica Kingsley.

Bion, W. R. (1959). *Experiences in Groups and Other Papers*. New York: Basic Books.

Bion, W. R. (1962). *Learning from Experience*. London: Heinemann.

Bion, W. R. (1967). *Second Thoughts*. London: Maresfield Reprints.

Biran, H. (2003). The difficulty of transforming terror into dialogue. *Group Analysis, 36*(4): 490–502.

Bleger, J. (1967). *Simbiosis y ambigüedad. Estudio psicoanalítico*. Buenos Aires: Paidós. [English translation: Symbiosis and ambiguity: A psychoanalytic study, J. Churcher & L. Bleger (Eds.), J. Churcher, L. Bleger, & S. Rogers (Trans.). London: Routledge, 2013.]

Bollas, C. (1987). *The Shadow of the Object: Psychoanalysis of the Unthought Known*. New York: Columbia University Press.

Bonaventure des Periers (1843). *Les nouvelles récréations et joyeux devis* (New recreations and joyous games). Paris: Gosselin.

Bourdieu, P. (1996). *The Rules of Art: Genesis and Structure of the Literary Field*, S. Emanuel (Trans.). Stanford, CA: Stanford University Press.

Bourdieu, P. (2000). *Pascalian Meditations*. Stanford, CA: Stanford University Press.

Brailey, K., Vasterling, J. J., Proctor, S. P., Constans, J. I., & Friedman, M. J. (2007). PTSD symptoms, life events, and unit cohesion in U.S. soldiers: baseline findings from the neurocognition deployment health study. *Journal of Trauma Stress*, 20(4): 495–503.

Brandes, S. (1983). Jewish-American dialect jokes and Jewish-American identity, *Jewish Social Studies*, 45: 233–240.

Brewer, D. (2003). The interpretation of fairy tales. In: H. E. Davidson & A. Chaudhri (Eds.), *A Companion to the Fairy Tale* (pp. 16–37). Cambridge: D. S. Brewer.

Brown, D. (1994). Self development through subjective interaction: a fresh look at 'ego training in action'. In: D. Brown & L. Zinkin (Eds.), *The Psyche and the Social World* (pp. 80–98). London: Jessica Kingsley.

Brown, D. (2001). A contribution to the understanding of the social unconscious. *Group Analysis*, 34(1): 29–38.

Browne, T., Hull, L., Horn, O., Jones, M., Murphy, D., Fear. N. T., Greenberg, N., French, C., Rona, R. J., Wessely, S., & Hotopf, M. (2007). Explanations for the increase in mental health problems in UK reserve forces who have served in Iraq. *British Journal of Psychiatry, 190*: 484–489.

Buck, W. (2000). *Mahabharata*. CA: University of California.

Butler J. (1990). *Bodies That Matter: On The Discursive Limit of Sex*. New York: Routledge.

Campbell, J. (2008). *The Hero with a Thousand Faces* (3rd edn). Novato, CA: New World Library.

Canetti, E. (1973). *Crowds and Power*, C. Stewart (Trans.). New York: Continuum.

Carsch, H. (1968). The role of the devil in Grimms' tales: an exploration of the content and function of popular tales. *Social Research* 35(3): 466–499.

Cavanagh, S. L., Failler, A., & Hurst, R. A. J. (Eds.) (2013). *Skin, Culture and Psychoanalysis*. London: Palgrave Macmillan.

Chodorow, N. (1978). *The Reproduction of Mothering*. Berkeley, CA: University of California Press.

Chodorow, N. (1989). *Feminism and Psychoanalytic Theory*. New Haven, CT: Yale University Press.
Chodorow, N. (1999). *The Power of Feelings: Personal Meaning in Psychoanalysis, Gender, and Culture*. New Haven, CT: Yale University Press.
Cox, M. R. (1893). *Cinderella*. London: David Nutt.
Dalal, F. (1998). *Taking the Group Seriously*. London: Jessica Kingsley.
Dalal, F. (2001). The social unconscious: a post-Foulkesian perspective. *Group Analysis*, 34(4): 539–555.
Dana, N. (Ed.). (1998). *The Druze*. Ramat-Gan: Bar-Ilan University Press (in Hebrew).
Darwin, C. (1952). *The Expression of the Emotion in Man and Animals*. Chicago, IL: University of Chicago Press.
De Mente, B. L. (2009). *Why the Japanese Are a Superior People*. Phoenix, AZ: Phoenix Books.
Dégh, L. (1979). Grimm's "Household Tales" and its place in the household: the social relevance of a controversial classic. *Western Folklore*, 38(2): 83–103.
Demy, J. (Dir.) (1970). *Peau d'Âne* (film). Entertainment One Film.
Dodds, E. R. (1973). On misunderstanding the Oedipus Rex. In: *The Ancient Concept of Progress* (pp. 64–77). Oxford: Oxford University Press.
Dundes, A. (1964). *The Morphology of North American Indian Folktales*. FF communication, 195. Helsinki: Academia Scientiarium Fennica.
Dundes, A. (1975). *Analytic Essays in Folklore*. The Hague: Mouton.
Dundes, A. (1978). To love my father all: a psychoanalytic study of the folktale source of King Lear. In: *Essays in Folkloristics* (pp. 207–222). Bloomington, IN: Folklore Institute.
Dundes, A. (Ed.) (1982). *Cinderella: A Folklore Casebook*. New York: Garland.
Dundes, A. (1985). The J.A.P. and the J.A.M. in American folklore. *Journal of American Folklore*, 98(390): 456–475.
Dundes, A. (1987a). *Parsing through Customs—Essays by a Freudian Folklorist*. Madison, WI: University of Wisconsin Press.
Dundes, A. (1987b). The psychoanalytic study of the Grimms' tales with special reference to the maiden without hands (AT 706). *The Germanic Review: Literature, Culture, Theory*, 62(2): 50–65.
Dundes, A. (2002). Projective inversion in the ancient Egyptian "Tale of Two Brothers". *The Journal of American Folklore*: 115(457/458): 378–394.
Durkheim, E. (1971). *The Elementary Forms of the Religious Life*, J. W. Swain (Trans.). London: George Allen & Unwin.
Elias, N. (1994). *The Civilizing Process*. Oxford: Blackwell.

Elias, N. (1996). *The Germans: Power Struggles and the Development of Habitus in the Nineteenth and Twentieth Centuries*. Oxford: Polity Press.

El-Shamy, H. M. (1999). *Tales Arab Women Tell and the Behavioral Patterns They Portray*. Bloomington, IN: Indiana University Press.

Eriksen, C. (2007). Why do they burn the 'bush'? Fire, rural livelihoods and conversation in Zambia. *Geographical Journal, 173*: 242–256.

Fairbairn, W. R. D. (1952). Endopsychic structure considered in terms of object-relationships. In: *Psychoanalytic Studies of the Personality* (pp. 82–132). London: Routledge & Kegan Paul.

Falah, S. (1983). *The Shadow of a Voice*. Tel Aviv: Hakibutz Hameuchad (Hebrew, translated from Arabic by Naim Araidi).

Falah, S., & Shenhar, A. (Eds.) (1978). *Druze Folktales*. Jerusalem: The Hebrew University (Hebrew).

Falah-Faraj, J. (2005). *The Druze Woman*. Rishon Le Zion: Barkai (in Hebrew).

Fenster, T. S. (1982). Beaumanoir's La Manekine: kin d(r)ead: incest, doubling, and death. *American Imago, 39*: 41–58.

Ferenczi, S. (1950)[1912]. The symbolic representation of the pleasure and reality principles in the Oedipus myth. In: *Sex in Psychoanalysis* (pp. 253–269), E. Jones (Trans.). New York: Basic Books.

Firro, K. (2001). *The Druze in the Jewish State*. Leiden: E. J. Brill.

Foulkes, S. H. (1964). *Therapeutic Group Analysis*. London: George Allen & Unwin.

Foulkes, S. H. (1975). A short outline of the therapeutic process in group analytic psychotherapy. *Group Analysis, 8*: 59–63.

Foulkes, S. H. (1990). The group as a matrix of the individual's mental life. In: E. Foulkes (Ed.), *Selected Papers* (pp. 223–233). London: Karnac.

Frazer, J. G. (1922). *The Golden Bough: A Study of Magic and Religion*. Adelaide, Australia: University of Adelaide.

Freud, S. (with Breuer, J.) (1895d). *Studies on Hysteria*. *S. E., 2*. London: Hogarth.

Freud, S. (1896). The aetiology of hysteria. *S. E., 3*: 189–221. London: Hogarth.

Freud, S. (1913d). The occurrence in dreams of material from fairy tales. *S. E., 12*: 279–287. London: Hogarth.

Freud, S. (1915e). The unconscious. *S. E., 14*: 161–204. London: Hogarth.

Freud, S. (1918b). *From the History of an Infantile Neurosis*. *S. E., 17*: 1–124. London: Hogarth.

Freud, S. (1919h). The "uncanny". *S. E., 17*: 219–256. London: Hogarth.

Freud, S. (1921c). *Group Psychology and the Analysis of the Ego. S. E., 18*: 67–143. London: Hogarth.

Freud, S., & Oppenheim, D. E. (1958)[1911]. *Dreams in Folklore*. New York: International Universities Press.

Fruchtman, M., Ben-Natan, A., & Shani, N. (2001). *Milon Ariel ha-Mekif*. Tel-Aviv: Korim (in Hebrew).

Gammell, C. (2008). Arab culture: the insult of the shoe. *Telegraph*, 15 December. Accessed at: www.telegraph.co.uk/news/worldnews/middleeast/iraq/3776970/Arab-culture-the-insult-of-the-shoe.html, on 5 June 2016.

Gautam, K. S. (Ed.) (1990). *India Through the Ages*. New Delhi, India: Publication Division, Ministry of Information and Broadcasting, Government of India.

Gilbert, S. (1985). Life's empty pack: notes toward a literary daughteronomy. *Critical Inquiry*, 11(3): 355–384.

Goldberg, C. (1997). The donkey skin folktale cycle (AT510b). *Journal of American Folklore*, 110(435): 28–46.

Goldberg, C. (2005). Cannibalism. In: J. Garry & El-Shamy, H. (Eds.), *Archetypes and Motifs in Folklore and Literature* (pp. 227–230). New York: M. E. Sharpe.

Golec de Zavala, A., Cichocka, A., Eidelson, R., & Jayawickreme, N. (2009). Collective narcissism and its social consequences. *Journal of Personality and Social Psychology*, 97(6): 1074–1096.

Gooch, G. P., Ginsburg, M., Willoughby, L. A., Butler, E. M., Stirk, S. D., & Pascal, R. (Eds.) (1945). *The German Mind and Outlook*. London: Chapman & Hall.

Gorer, G. (1948). *The American People: A Study in National Character*. New York: W. W. Norton.

Gorer, G. (1949). *The People of Great Russia: A Psychological Study*. London: The Cresset Press.

Goudsblom, J. (1992). *Fire and Civilization*. London: Penguin.

Green, R. L. (2011). *Tales of Ancient Egypt*. Harmondsworth: Penguin.

Grimm, J., & Grimm, W. (1909–1914). *Household Tales*. New York: Harvard Classics.

Grotjahn, M. (1961). Jewish jokes and their relations to masochism. *Journal of the Hillside Hospital*, 10: 183–189.

Haimowits, M. (1976). *Loyal Guardians: Folk-tales of 13 Tellers*. IFA Publication 34. Haifa: The Museum of Folklore and Ethnology, the Israeli Folklore Archive (in Hebrew).

Harari, Y. N. (2015). *Sapiens: A Brief History of Humankind*. New York: HarperCollins.

Harshbarger, S. (2013). Grimm and grimmer: "Hansel and Gretel" and fairy tale nationalism. *Style*, 47(4): 490–508.

Henderson, J. L. (1984). *Cultural Attitudes in Psychological Perspective*. Toronto: Inner City Books.

Herman, J. L. (1992). *Trauma and Recovery*. New York: Basic Books.

Herodotus (1937). *The Histories*. New-York: Pantheon Books (translated from Greek by A. L. Purvis).

Holbek, B. (1998). *Interpretation of Fairy Tales: Danish Folklore in A European Perspective*. (FFC 239) Helsinki: Academia Scientiarum Fennica.

Hopper, E. (2001). The social unconscious: theoretical considerations. *Group Analysis, 34*(1): 9–27.

Hopper, E. (2003a) *Traumatic Experience in the Unconscious Life of Groups*. London: Jessica Kingsley.

Hopper, E. (2003b). *The Social Unconscious: Selected Papers*. London: Jessica Kingsley.

Hopper, E., & Weinberg, H. (Eds.) (2011). *The Social Unconscious in Persons, Groups, and Societies: Volume 1: Mainly Theory*. London: Karnac.

Hopper, E., & Weinberg, H. (Eds.) (2016). *The Social Unconscious in Persons, Groups, and Societies: Volume 2: Mainly Foundation Matrices*. London: Karnac.

Hopper, E., & Weinberg, H. (Eds.) (2017). *The Social Unconscious in Persons, Groups, and Societies: Volume 3: The Foundation Matrix Extended and Re-Configured*. London: Karnac.

Hughes, J. H., Cameron, F., Eldridge, R., Devon, M., Wessely, S., & Greenberg, N. (2005). Going to war does not have to hurt: preliminary findings from the British deployment to Iraq. *British Journal of Psychiatry, 186*: 536–537.

Ihms, S. M. (1975). The brothers Grimm and their collection of 'Kinder and Hausmärchen'. *Theoria: A Journal of Social and Political Theory, 45*: 41–54.

Jason, H. (1977). A model for narrative study in oral literature. In: H. Jason & D. Segal (Eds.), *Pattern in Oral Literature* (pp. 99–133) Paris: Mouton Publishers.

Jones, E. (1951). *Essays in Applied Psycho-analysis, II*. International Psycho-Analytical Library No. 41. London: Hogarth.

Jones, E. (1965). Psychoanalysis and folklore. In: A. Dundes (Ed.), *The Study of Folklore* (pp. 42–47). Englewood Cliffs, NJ: Prentice-Hall.

Jones, S. S. (1993). The innocent persecuted heroine genre: an analysis of its structure and themes. *Western Folklore, 52*(1): 13–41.

Joseph, B. (1985). Transference: the total situation. *International Journal of Psychoanalysis, 66*(4), 447–454.

Kaës, R., Missenard, A., Anzieu, D., Kaspi, A., Guillaumin, J., Bleger, J., & Jaques, E. (2013). *Crise, rupture et dépassement* (Crisis, rupture and overtaking) (2nd edn). Paris: Dunod.

Kafka, F. (1966). *In the Penal Colony*. Cambridge: Cambridge University Press.

Katz, N., & Katz, E. (1971). Tradition and adaptation in American Jewish humor. *Journal of American Folklore, 84*: 215–220.

Klein, M. (1946). Notes on some schizoid mechanisms. In: *The Writings of Melanie Klein, Vol. 3, Envy and Gratitude and Other Works* (pp. 1–24). London: Hogarth Press.

Klein, M. (1984). *Envy and Gratitude and Other Works 1946–1963*. London: Hogarth Press.

Knedler, J. W. (1937). The girl without hands: a comparative study in folklore and romance. Unpublished Doctoral thesis, Harvard University. In: A. Dundes (Ed.) (1987) The psychoanalytic study of the Grimms' tales with special reference to the maiden without hands (ATU 706). *The Germanic Review: Literature, Culture, Theory, 62*(2): 61.

Koenigsberg, R. (1996). *Hitler's Body and the Body Politic: The Psychosomatic Source of Culture*. New York: Library of Social Science.

Kohn, H. (1950). Romanticism and the rise of German nationalism. *Review of Politics, 12*(4): 443–472.

Kohut, H. (1977). *The Restoration of the Self*. New York: International Universities Press.

Kuipers, G. (2013). The rise and decline of national habitus: Dutch cycling culture and the shaping of national similarity. *European Journal of Social Theory, 16*(1): 17–35.

Lacan, J. (2007). *The Seminar of Jacques Lacan. Book XIX. The Other Side of Psychoanalysis*, R. Grigg (Trans.), J.-A. Miller (Ed.). New York: Norton.

Lakoff, G., & Johnson, M. (1980). *Metaphors We Live By*. Chicago, IL: University of Chicago Press.

Lawrence, W. G. (Ed.) (1998). *Social Dreaming @ Work*. London: Karnac.

Layish, A. (1982). *Marriage, Divorce and Succession in the Druze Family*. Leiden: E. J. Brill.

Le Roy, J. (1994). Group analysis and culture. In: D. Brown & L. Zinkin (Eds.), *The Psyche and the Social World* (pp. 180–201). London: Jessica Kingsley.

Lévi-Strauss, C. (1995). *Myth and Meaning*. New York: Schocken Books.

Levy, A. (2003). Notes on Jewish-Muslim relationships: revisiting the vanishing Moroccan Jewish community. *Cultural Anthropology, 18*(4): 365–397.

Lewis, C. S. (1977). *The Allegory of Love: A Study in Medieval Tradition*. Oxford: Oxford University Press.

Librecht, S. (1992). 'The Berries' Girl'. In: *"It's Greek to Me"*, *She Said to Him* (pp. 61–82). Tel Aviv: Keter (in Hebrew).

Lothspeich, P. (2009). *Epic Nation: Reimagining the Mahabharata in the Age of the Empire*. Oxford: Oxford University Press.

Martin, E. (1990). Toward an anthropology of immunology: the body as nation state. *Medical Anthropology Quarterly*, 4(4): 410–426.

McDougall, J. (1998). *Theaters of the Mind*. New York: Basic Books.

Mills, M. A. (1982). A Cinderella variant in the context of Muslim women's ritual. In: A. Dundes (Ed.), *Cinderella: A Folklore Casebook* (pp. 185–189). New York: Garland.

Milo, H., & Raufman, R. (2014). The princess in the wooden body: Israeli oral versions of "The Maiden in the Chest" (ATU 510B*) in light of incest victims' blogs. *Journal of American Folklore*, 127(503): 50–71.

Miron, Y., Shehadi-Mishaiel, C., & Ahmad Masarwah, N. (2002). *Pomegranate Seed: Arab Women's Folktales from Israel*. Givat-Haviva: Jewish–Arab Centre for Peace.

Muhawi, I. (2001). Gender and disguise in the Arabic Cinderella: a study in the cultural dynamics of representation. *Fabula*, 42: 263–283.

Musolff, A. (2010). *Metaphor, Nation and the Holocaust: The Concept of the Body Politic*. New York: Routledge.

Nacht, J. (1915). The symbolism of the shoe with special reference to Jewish sources. *Jewish Quarterly Review*, 6: 1–22.

Neri, C., Pines, M., & Friedman, R. (2002). *Dreams in Group Psychotherapy: Theory and Technique*. London: Jessica Kingsley.

Nicholson, H. B. (1971). *Handbook of Middle American Indians*. University of Texas Press.

Nicolaisen, W. F. H. (1993). Perspective on the innocent persecuted heroine in fairy tales. *Western Folklore*, 52(1): 61–71.

Noy, D. (1966). *Moroccan Jewish Folktales*. New York: Herzl Press.

Ogden, T. H. (1989). On the concept of an autistic-contiguous position. *International Journal of Psychoanalysis*, 70 127–140.

Ogden, T. H. (2010). Why read Fairbairn? *International Journal of Psychoanalysis*, 91: 101–118.

Parsons, L. (2000). *The Druze between Palestine and Israel 1947–49*. Basingstoke: Macmillan Press.

Perco, D. (1993). Female initiation in Northern Italian versions of "Cinderella", *Western Folklore*, 52(1): 73–84.

Perrault, C. (1697). *Histoires ou Contes du Temps Passe: Avec des Moralites*. Paris: Marpon and Flammarion.

Pines, M. (1998). *Circular Reflections*. London: Jessica Kingsley.

Pines, M. (2003). Social brain and social group: how mirroring connects people. *Group Analysis, 36*(4): 507–513.
Pisani, R. A. (1993). Neuroses and group culture in Southern Italy. *Group Analysis, 26*, 239–249.
Powell, A. (1982). Metaphors in group analysis. *Group Analysis, 15*(2): 127–135.
Propp, V. (1968). *Morphology of the Folktale*, Austin, TX: University of Texas Press.
Racker, H. (1957). The meaning and uses of countertransference. *Psychoanalytic Quarterly, 26:* 303–357.
Rank, O. (1912). *Hands Das Inzest-Motif in Dichtung und Sage*, Leipzig: Deuticke.
Rank, O. (1929). *The Birth Trauma*. London: Kegan Paul, Trench, Trubner.
Raufman, R. (2008). Wandering through the dark forest: dreams and fairy tales in a group workshop. *Funzione Gamma Journal, 22*. Available at: www.funzionegamma.it/wp-content/uploads/wandering22e.pdf.
Raufman, R. (2011). Defending the house, relating to the neighbors: the Druze versions of ATU 123 "The Wolf and the Kids". *Folklore, 122*(3): 250–263.
Raufman, R. (2012). Realizations of idiomatic expressions in Israeli oral wonder tales. *Fabula, 53*(1/2): 20–45.
Raufman, R. (2014). "Asked for her hand"—the realization of idiomatic expressions in dreams and fairy tales in relational group therapy: whose needs are these anyway? *Group, 38*(3): 217–228.
Raufman, R. (2015). Aspects of the social unconscious reflected in traditional folktales: the case of the Druze community in Israel. In: E. Hopper & H. Weinberg (Eds.), *The Social Unconscious in Person, Groups, and Societies, Vol. 2: Mainly Foundation Matrices* (pp. 43–58). London: Karnac.
Raufman, R. (in press). The affinity between incest and women's mutilation in the feminine Druze versions of the maiden without hands: an international motif in a local context. *Marvels and Tales*.
Raufman, R., & Weinberg, H. (2014). Two forms of blindness in the social unconscious as expressed in literary texts. *Group Analysis, 47*(2): 159–174.
Raufman, R., & Weinberg, H. (2016a). Early mother–son relationships, primary levels of mental organization and the foundation matrix as expressed in fairy tales: the case of the "Jewish Mother". *Group Analysis, 49*(2): 149–163.
Raufman, R., & Weinberg, H. (2016b). "To enter one's skin": the concrete and symbolic functions of the skin in the social unconscious, as expressed in fairy tales and group therapy. *International Journal of Group Psychotherapy, 66*(2): 205–224.

Raufman, R., & Yigael, Y. (2010). "Feeling good in your own skin". Part I: Primary levels of mental organization. *American Journal of Psychoanalysis, 70*: 361–385.

Raufman, R., & Yigael, Y. (2011). "Feeling good in your own skin". Part II: Idiomatic expressions—the language's way to connect with the primary levels of mental organization. *American Journal of Psychoanalysis, 71*: 16–36.

Raufman, R., & Yigael, Y. (in press). The primary psyche from the wonder–tales' point of view. *American Journal of Psychoanalysis*.

Ribuoli, P., & Robbiani, M. (1992). *Frog. Art, Legend, History*, J. Gilbert (Trans.). Boston, MA: Bulfinch Press, Little, Brown.

Robins, R. W. (2005). The nature of personality: genes, culture, and national character. *Science, 310*(5745): 62–63.

Röhrich, L. (1991). *Folktales and Reality*. Indianapolis, IN: Indiana University Press.

Rooth, A. B. (1951). *The Cinderella Cycle*. Lund: C. W. K. Gleerup.

Rusch-Feja, D. (1995). *The Portrayal of the Maturation Process of Girl Figures in Selected Tales of the Brothers Grimm*. Frankfurt: P. Lang.

Rutan, S. J., Stone, N. W., & Shay, J. J. (2014). *Psychodynamic Group Psychotherapy* (5th edn). New York: Guilford Press.

Saadon, H. (2004). *Morocco*. Jerusalem: Ministry of Education (in Hebrew).

Saramago, J. (1997). *Blindness*. London: Harville Press.

Schachter, D. L., & Moscovitch, M. (1984). Infants, amnesia and dissociable memory systems. In: M. Moscovitch (Ed.), *Infant Memory* (pp. 173–216). New York: Plenum.

Schlachet, P. J. (1995). The dream in group therapy: a reappraisal of unconscious process in groups. *GROUP, 16*(4), 196–209.

Schlauch, M. (1969). *Chaucer's Constance and Accused Queens*. New York: Gordian Press.

Schneider, S., & Weinberg, H. (Eds.) (2003). *The Large Group Re-Visited*. London: Jessica Kingsley.

Scholz, R. (2014). (Foundation-)Matrix reloaded—some remarks on a useful concept and its pitfalls. *Group Analysis*: 47(3): 201–212.

Scholz, R. (2017). The fluid and the solid—or the dynamic and the static: some further thoughts about the conceptualization of "foundation matrices" processes of "the social unconscious" and/or "large group identities". In: E. Hopper & H. Weinberg (Eds.), *The Social Unconscious in Persons, Groups, and Societies: Volume III. The Foundation Matrix Extended and Re-configured*. London: Karnac (in press).

Segal, H. (1957). Notes on symbol formation. *International Journal of Psychoanalysis, 38*: 391–397.

Shakespeare, W. (1988). *Four Tragedies: Hamlet, Othello, King Lear, Macbeth*. New York: Bantam Books.
Shenhar, A. (1982). *Israeli Folktales*. Tel Aviv: Ts'erikover (in Hebrew).
Shenhar, A. (1987). 'The Maiden Without Hands' folktale. In: *Jewish and Israeli Folklore* (pp. 47–68). New Delhi: South Asian Publishers.
Singer, T., & Kimbles, S. (Eds.) (2004). *The Cultural Complex: Contemporary Jungian Perspectives on Psyche and Society*. London: Brunner-Routledge.
Staples, A. (1998). *From Good Goddess to Vestal Virgins: Sex and Category in Roman Religion*. New York: Routledge.
Steiner, R. (1911). *Rosenkreuzerisches Weistum in der Märchendichtung*, Einzelausgabe, Dornach.
Stone, W. N. (2005). Group-as-a-whole: a self psychological perspective. *Group*, *29*: 239–255.
Symington, N. (1983). The analyst's act of freedom as agent of therapeutic change. *International Journal of Psychoanalysis*, *10*(3): 283–291.
Tajfel, H. (1982). *Social Identity and Intergroup Relations*. Cambridge: Cambridge University Press.
Tatar, M. (1987). *The Hard Facts of the Grimms' Fairy Tales*. Princeton, NJ: Princeton University Press.
Tatar, M. (1992). *Off With Their Heads! Fairy Tales and the Culture of Childhood*. Princeton, NJ: Princeton University Press.
Thompson, S. (1955–1958). *Motif-Index of Folk-Literature: A Classification of Narrative Element in Folktales, Ballads, Myths, Fables, Medieval Romances, Exempla, Fabliaux, Jest-Books and Local Legend*. Bloomington, IN: Indiana University Press.
Tssab, A. (1998). The force to change Druze women's status. In: N. Dana (Ed.), *The Druze* (pp. 119–123). Ramat-Gan: Bar-Ilan University Press (in Hebrew).
Tubert-Oklander, J. (2017). The inner organization of the matrix. In: E. Hopper & H. Weinberg (Eds.), *The Social Unconscious in Persons, Groups and Societies: Volume III. The Foundation Matrix Extended and Re-configured*. London: Karnac (in press).
Tylor, E. B. (1958). *Primitive Culture, Volumes 1–2*. New York: Harper.
Ulman, M. (1996). *Appreciating Dreams: A Group Approach*. Thousand Oaks, CA: Sage.
Ulnik, J. (2007). *Skin in Psychoanalysis*. London: Karnac.
Uther, H. J. (2004). *The Types of International Folktales: A Classification and Bibliography, Based on the System of Antti Aarne and Stith Thompson*, 293–296. Helsinki: Suomalainen Tiedeakatemia, Academia Scientiarum Fennica.
Volkan, V. (2001). Transgenerational transmissions and chosen traumas: an aspect of large-group identity. *Group-Analysis*, *34*(1): 79–97.

Wardi, D. (1992). *Memorial Candles: Children of the Holocaust*. London: Routledge.
Warner, M. (1994). *From the Beast to the Blond-On Fairy Tales and Their Tellers*. New York: Farrar, Straus and Giroux.
Weinberg, H. (2007). So what is this social unconscious anyway? *Group Analysis*, 40(3): 307–322.
Weinberg, H. (2009). The Israeli social unconscious. *Mikbaz, the Israeli Journal of Group Psychotherapy*: 14(1): 11–28 (in Hebrew).
Weinberg, H. (2015). The group as an inevitable relational field, especially in times of conflict. In: R. Grossmark & F. Wright (Eds.), *The One and the Many: Relational Approaches to Group Psychotherapy* (pp. 38–56). New York: Routledge.
Weinberg, H. (2017). The social unconscious of Israeli Jews described and analysed by an Israeli living in North America. In: E. Hopper & H. Weinberg (Eds.), *The Social Unconscious in Persons, Groups, and Societies. Volume III. The Foundation Matrix Extended and Re-configured*. London: Karnac (in press).
Weiss, M. (2002). The body of the nation: terrorism and the embodiment of nationalism in contemporary Israel. *Anthropological Quarterly*, 75(1): 37–62.
Wilke, G. (2007). Second generation perpetrator symptoms in groups. *Group Analysis*, 40(4): 429–447.
Winnicott, D. W. (1945). Primitive emotional development. *International Journal of Psychoanalysis*, 26: 137–145.
Winnicott, D. W. (1957). *The Child and the Outside World*. London: Tavistock.
Wolfenstein, M. (1963). Two types of Jewish mothers. In: M. Mead & M. Wolfenstein (Eds.), *Childhood in Contemporary Cultures* (pp. 424–440). Chicago, IL: The University of Chicago Press.
Yair, G. (2017). The national habitus: steps toward reintegrating sociology and group analysis. In: E. Hopper & H. Weinberg: (Eds.), *The Social Unconscious in Persons, Groups, and Societies: Volume III. The Foundation Matrix Extended and Re-configured*. London: Karnac (in press).
Yalom, I. (1995). *The Theory and Practice of Group Psychotherapy* (4th edn). New York: Basic Books.
Yalom, I. D., & Leszcz, M. (2005). *The Theory & Practice of Group Psychotherapy* (5th edn). New York: Basic Books.
Ziaul, H., & Fahmida Kabir, F. (2013). The concept of blindness in Sophocles' *King Oedipus* and Arthur Miller's *Death of a Salesman*. *International Journal of Applied Linguistics & English Literature*, 2(3): 112–119.

Zipes, J. (1977). The revolutionary rise of the romantic fairy tale in Germany. *Studies in Romanticism*, *16*(4): 409–450.

Zipes, J. (1991). *Fairy Tales and the Art of Subversion*, New York: Routledge.

Zipes, J. (1995). *Creative Storytelling: Building Community, Changing Lives*. New York: Routledge.

Zoran, R. (2000). *The Third Voice.* Jerusalem: Carmel (in Hebrew).

INDEX

Aarne, A., 74, 97, 99, 125, 138–139
Ahmad Masarwah, N., 33
Alexander, T., 101
Allen, W., 10
anxiety, xiv, 11, 39, 51–52, 64, 81, 93
   attacks, 51
   castration, 19
   personal, 32
   provoking, 93
   psychical, 52
   psychological, 3
   universal, 68–69
Anzieu, D., xiv, xxv–xxvi, 39–40, 42–46, 49–50, 52, 54–55, 138
Aristotle, 93
Atashe, Z., 34
awareness, xxviii–xxix, 27, 69, 84, 91–93 *see also*: self

Bacchilega, C., 30, 106
Bahloul, J., 129
Bargh, J. A., 137
Bar-Itzhak, H., 101, 105

Basile, G., 98, 138
Bauer, P., xix
behavior(al), xviii, 25–27, 44, 73, 87–88, 95, 113, 117, 134, 138
   dimensions, xxviii
   dominant, 26
   heroine's, 47, 138
   masturbatory, 24
   social, 120
   somatic, 20
   structure, xxix
Ben-Amos, D., xx, 12, 74
Ben-Dor, G., 34
Benedict, R., 9, 11
Benjamin, J., 7, 12
Ben-Natan, A., 125
Berandt, C., 27
Berger, M., 75
Berman, A., 75
Bettelheim, B., 47, 100, 105
Bick, E., 39, 46–47
Billow, R. M., 23
Bion, W. R., xxiii–xxiv, 23, 45, 93

Biran, H., xxiv
Bleger, J., xxiii, 50
blind(ness), 64, 79–80, 83–88, 90–93, 140 *see also*: self
  aspects of, 83–84
  completely, 79
  concrete, 62, 88
  expressions of, 84
  eye, xxv, 59, 63, 88
  functions of, 84, 90
  inexplicable, 87
  issue of, 91
  metaphorically, 62, 84–85
  person, 88
  physical, 62, 85
  psychological, 88
  role of, 90
  white, 83
Bollas, C., xxviii
Bonaventure des Periers, 98
Bourdieu, P., xxi, 74
Brailey, K., 138
Brandes, S., 12
Breuer, J., 24
Brewer, D., 71
Brown, D., 52, 105
Browne, T., 139
Buck, W., 84
Burrows, L., 137
Butler, E. M., 9
Butler, J., 106

Cameron, F., 139
Campbell, J., 127
Canetti, E., 63, 65
Carsch, H., 35
Cavanagh, S. L., 53
Chen, M., 137
Chodorow, N., 6–7
Cichocka, A., 74
conscious(ness), xix, xxii, xxvii, 3, 9, 20, 23, 43, 66, 69, 93, 134 *see also*: unconscious
  ego, 127
  elements, xxvii
  emergence of, 80
  higher, 69
  level, 13, 114
  meanings, 53–54
  mind, xiv
  non-, xx, 134
  pre-, xx, 134
  products, 86
  self-, 67
  unity of, 89
Constans, J. I., 138
containing, xxiv, 40, 42–43, 46, 49–50, 52, 69, 106–107 *see also*: self
  function, 47, 52
  maternal figure, 47
  mother, xxiii
  –protective feature, 55
  skin, 43–44
Cox, M. R., 97, 107

Dalal, F., xxi, 75, 105
Dana, N., 33
Darwin, C., 128
De Mente, B. L., 73
Dégh, L., 65, 67–68, 139
Demy, J., 37, 49
denial, 83–85, 92–93
dependence, xx, 10, 33, 47, 106
  of abstract constructions, xiv
  bourgeoisie, 71
  failed, 48
development(al), xii, xix, 6, 8, 70, 130 *see also*: self
  delays, x
  of democratic values, 72
  disturbances, 48
  early, 1, 3, 22, 118
  of envy, 59
  human, 39, 81–82, 92, 117, 128
  of human society, 77
  individual, xxix, 39, 77, 120
  infant's, xxiii
  of mankind, 118
  normal, 6
  period, 39
  primary, 5
  process, 7

proper, 45
psychic, xxi
  life, 5
speech, 119
stage, xxix, 3, 22
step, xxix
Devon, M., 139
Dodds, E. R., 140
dream, 15–16, 19–21, 23, 25–27, 35, 64, 66 *see also*: matrix
  collective, xxvi
  language, 127
  material, 25
  narrative, 26–27
  social, 20
  -telling, 20, 25, 32
  time, 133
Dundes, A., xvii, xx, 9–12, 18–20, 24, 29, 35, 47, 65–66, 74, 97, 102, 107, 138
Durkheim, E., 67

ego, xxv, 39–40, 43–45, 55 *see also*: conscious
  body, xxv, 39
  -centric, 4, 20
  group, 50, 55
  psychic, 39
  skin-, xiv–xxvi, 38–40, 43–45, 48–50, 52–55, 75, 138–139
  super-, xiv
  thinking, 39
Eidelson, R., 74
Eldridge, R., 139
Elias, N., xxi, 71–72, 75, 118–119
El-Shamy, H. M., 47
envy, xi, xxiv, 10, 57–59, 62–64, 75–77, 80–82, 104, 112, 123–124, 131, 134–135
  centrality of, 81
  impulses, 81
  uncontrolled, 62
Eriksen, C., 118

Fahmida Kabir, F., 140
Failler, A., 53

Fairbairn, W. R. D., xx
Falah, S., 138
Falah-Faraj, J., 32
fantasy, 6, 9, 18, 29–30, 39, 45–47, 50, 55, 75–76, 120, 128, 138 *see also*: unconscious
  body, 55
  early, 46
  elements, 8
  imagined, 18
  infantile, 89
  level, 29
  masturbatory, 24
  of nationalism, xxvi
  totalitarian, xxvi
Fear, N. T., 139
Fenster, T. S., 19
Ferenczi, S., 93
Firro, K., 34
Foulkes, S. H., x, xvii–xviii, xxi, 23, 46, 50–51, 54, 71–72
Frazer, J. G., 119
French, C., 139
Freud, S., xii, xvii, xx, xxiv–xxv, xxix, 9, 18, 20–22, 24, 58, 64–66, 74, 115
Friedman, M. J., 138
Friedman, R., 20
Fruchtman, M., 125

Gammell, C., 100
Gautam, K. S., 118
Gilbert, S., 32
Ginsburg, M., 9
Goldberg, C., 10, 47, 99
Golec de Zavala, A., 74
Gooch, G. P., 9
Gorer, G., 9
Goudsblom, J., 119–120
Green, R. L., 98
Greenberg, N., 139
Grimm, J., 17–18, 58–59, 63–68, 70–72, 74–77, 81, 98–99, 127–128, 134, 139
Grimm, W., xv, 17–18, 58–59, 63–68, 70–72, 74–77, 81, 98–99, 127–128, 134, 139

Grotjahn, M., 11–12
Guillaumin, J., 50
guilt, xv, 5, 10, 24–25, 81, 91–93
　feelings, 11, 25, 91
　-free, 91
Gutmann, D., 75

habitus, xxi–xxii, 71–72
Haimowits, M., 114
Harari, Y. N., 133
Harshbarger, S., 65, 67
Henderson, J. L., xviii
Herman, J. L., 30, 48
Herodotus, 99
Holbek, B., xix, xxix
Hopper, E., xii, xvii–xx, xxvi, 13, 44, 54, 67, 77, 134
Horn, O., 139
Hotopf, M., 139
Hughes, J. H., 139
Hull, L., 139
Hurst, R. A. J., 53

identity, 7, 42, 48–49, 99, 103, 107
　collective, 67
　dilemmas, 38
　dystonic, 49
　establishment of, 49
　feminine, 41, 107
　gender, 6–7
　group, 54
　injury, 48
　issues of, 34
　legal, 28
　masculine, 6–7
　national, xxvi, 55, 67, 82, 134
　proof, 97
　sense of, 10, 42, 47, 49, 53
　social, 55–56
　test, 105
　transformation, 48
　true, 42, 107
Ihms, S. M., 65
incest, 18–19, 24, 27, 29–32, 37–38, 47–49, 102, 105, 138
Israeli Defence Forces (IDF), 34

Israeli Folktale Archive (IFA), 2, 41, 59, 86, 100, 123

Jaques, E., 50
Jason, H., xxviii
Jayawickreme, N., 74
jealousy, 3–4, 57–58, 61, 63, 70, 81–82, 85, 125
Johnson, M., xxv
Jones, E., 102, 127
Jones, M., 139
Jones, S. S., 30–32
Joseph, B., 23

Kaës, R., 50
Kafka, F., xiv–xv
Kaspi, A., 50
Katz, E., 12
Katz, N., 12
Kimbles, S., xviii
Klein, M., xxii, xxiv, 20, 81
Knedler, J. W., 19
Koenigsberg, R., xxvi
Kohn, H., 65
Kohut, H., 89
Kuipers, G., 9

Lacan, J., xxii, 50, 140
Lakoff, G., xxv
Lawrence, W. G., 20, 27
Layish, A., 33
Le Roy, J., xxi, 54
Leszcz, M., 50
Lévi-Strauss, C., 76, 80, 117
Levy, A., 129
Lewis, C. S., 140
Librecht, S., 90
Lothspeich, P., 84
lust, 47, 115–118, 122
　fire of, 112, 114–117, 120, 122
　unrestrained, 115

Martin, E., xxvi, 55
matrix, 46
　foundation, xii, xvi–xix, xxi, xxiii–xxiv, xxvii, xxx, 2, 10, 13,

16–17, 19, 28, 35, 58, 70–72, 82, 84, 90, 105, 120–121
fundamental mental, xviii
group, 20, 135
personal, xii
social, xxi
dreaming (SDM), 20
McDougall, J., xxiv, 5
metaphor(ic), xxiii, xxv–xxxvi, 4–6, 14, 16, 34–35, 40, 42, 44, 55, 85, 93, 112, 129–130 *see also*: blind
aspects, xv, xviii
concept, xvi
denial, 85
expression, xxiv, 6, 13, 88
ideas, xv, 42, 96
idioms, 20, 103
level, 6, 14, 84, 88, 115
meaning, 2, 87, 103, 131
microcosms, 102
organic, 50
organism, xxvi, 54
Mills, M. A., 104
Milo, H., 48–49
Miron, Y., 33
Missenard, A., 50
Moscovitch, M., xxii
Muhawi, I., 47, 99, 107
Murphy, D., 139
Musolff, A., xxvi
myth(ology), xxx, 3, 9, 13, 28, 64–65, 68, 73–76, 80, 85–86, 93, 106, 116–121, 127–128, 133–134
ancient, 119
Australian, 133
Egyptian, 119, 128
figures, 76
Graiai, 74–75
Greek, 74, 85, 119
imagined, 133
Inca, 4, 10
Indian, 84
Israeli, 12
Italian, 119
Japanese, 76
national, 133

Nordic, 139
oedipal, 80, 93
thought, 84

Nacht, J., 96, 107
Neri, C., 20
Nicholson, H. B., 121
Nicolaisen, W. F. H., 99
Noy, D., 129

object, xxiii, 9, 47, 114 *see also*: self
concrete, 9, 127
erotic, 107
external, 47
function, 47
good, 81
inferior, 103
of interest, x
internal, xx
lost, xxiv
love, 4
magical, 114
mediating, xi
observing, 23
relations, 23, 42
oedipal *see also*: myth
components, 101, 105
desires, 18, 47, 105
period, 6
pre-, 6
stage, 4
Oedipus, 65, 85, 93, 140
Ogden, T. H., xx, xxii–xxiii, 39
Oppenheim, D. E., 66

Parsons, L., 34–35
Pascal, R., 9
Perco, D., 47
Perrault, C., 47, 65, 98
persecuted, 34–35, 65, 81, 126
aspect, 10
community, 35
heroine, 30, 34–35, 97, 105
women, 10, 35
Pines, M., xxiv, 20, 51
Pisani, R. A., 10

Powell, A., xxv
process(es), xix–xx, xxiv, 6, 13, 26–27, 39, 47, 53, 72, 91, 122 *see also*: development, unconscious
    adaptation, xxviii
    analytic, 25
    biological, xi
    central, 9
    civilizing, 118, 120, 122
    complicated, 27
    crucial, 39
    encapsulation, xx
    evolutionary, 127
    fusionary, xi
    gradual, 108
    group, 21–24, 27, 29, 84, 90, 92–93
    historical, 69
    of individuation, 69–70
    industrialization, ix
    inner, 122
    maturation, 69
        –individuation, 76
    mental, x, xxii, 40
    methodological, 59
    ongoing, 12
    parallel, ix, 25–26
    primary, xvi
    psychological, 48
    secondary, xxii, 43
    sensorial, 101
    separation, 5–7, 12
    social, xxv, 72, 74
    thought, xvi, xxvii–xxix, 3–4, 43, 59, 84, 115, 120, 125, 127–128
    universal, 13
Proctor, S. P., 138
Propp, V., xx–xxi, xxviii, 73–74, 76
psychic(al), xxv *see also*: anxiety, development
    apparatus, xxv, 39
    contents, 45
    envelope, 39, 47
    instances, 50
    investments, 53
    level, 45
    life, 5, 39
    liveliness, 112
    mechanism, 44–45
    organization, xxii
    separation, xxi
    skin, 50
        group, 50
        social, 50
    topography, 52
    unity, xvii

Racker, H., 23
Rank, O., xxi, 18
Raufman, R., xvi, xviii–xix, xxii, xxiv–xxv, 1, 15, 20, 22, 29–32, 34, 37, 48–49, 83, 137
resonance, 42, 50–54, 56–58, 74, 93
Ribuoli, P., 128
ritual, 19, 50, 58, 107, 119–121
Robbiani, M., 128
Robins, R. W., 9
Röhrich, L., xix
Rona, R. J., 139
Rooth, A. B., 97
Rusch-Feja, D., 69–70
Rutan, S. J., 50

Saadon, H., 129–130
Saramago, J., 83
Schachter, D. L., xxii
Schlachet, P. J., 26
Schlauch, M., 138
Schneider, S., 54, 56
Scholz, R., xviii, xxi
Segal, H., xxiv
self, xxiii, xxv–xxvi, 7–8, 39, 44–48, 54–55 *see also*: conscious
    -assertion, 70
    -awareness, 69
    -blinding, 65
    -centered, 25
    -childish, 45
    -contained, 75
    -critical, 51
    -criticism, 73
    -development, 69, 139
    -evident, 69

-government, 69
group, 50
-image, 49
-in-relation, 7
-mastery, 118
mental, 45
-mockery, 12
-object, 50, 91
-psychology, 89
-sacrifice, 3–4
somatic, 45
-worth, 72
sensorial, 38–40
　aspect, 39–40, 43
　body, 49
　experience, xiv, 40, 44, 58, 88
　inter-, 40
　level, xxvii
　manner, 42
　organs, 44
　pictorial–, 112
　processes, 101
　reactions, 38
　realm, 43
　somatic
　　aspects, xviii
　　experiences, xxii, xxviii
　understanding, xxx
sexual(ity), 24, 35, 50, 95, 138
　abuse, 30, 48
　advances, 19
　conceptualization, 32
　contents, 21
　desire, 24, 108
　excitation, 40
　explanations, 19
　fear, 127
　hetero-, 102
　intercourse, 130
　relations, 28–29, 100, 105, 107
　sinning, 24
　symbolism, 107
Shakespeare, W., 57, 82
Shani, N., 125
Shay, J. J., 50
Shehadi-Mishaiel, C., 33

Shenhar, A., 17, 138
Singer, T., xviii
Staples, A., 121
Steiner, R., xxix, 120
Stirk, S. D., 9
Stone, N. W., 50
Stone, W. N., 50
structure, xxi, xxviii–xxix, 105, 120
　see also: behavior
　class, 105
　collective memories, 67
　family, 54
　infra-, 139
　logical, xvii
　power, 105–106
　reflexive, 46
　sensation, x
　social, xxi–xxii, 105–106
symbol(-ic), xiv, xx, xxii, xxvi–xxvii,
　　5, 8–9, 18, 55, 58, 65–66, 75,
　　99–100, 105, 107, 127–129 *see also*:
　　sexual
　of abundance, 128
　capabilities, 128
　concept of, xxiv, 43
　description, xix
　equation, xx
　equivalent, 102
　erotic, 70
　father, 26
　fertility, 128
　function, xxiv
　group, 50
　of hope, 130
　idiom, 47
　inferences, xxvi
　interpretation, 97
　language, 135
　letters, xiv
　level, 96
　linguistic, xv
　meaning, 9, 106, 108, 128
　–metaphoric aspects, xviii
　offensive, 101
　pre-, xxiii
　realms, xvi, 8

representations, 43, 49
verbal expression, 3
Symington, N., 23

Tajfel, H., 74
Tatar, M., 138
Thompson, S., 18, 74, 96–97, 99, 125, 138–139
Tssab, A., 33
Tubert-Oklander, J., xxiii
Tylor, E. B., xxix, 120

Ullman, M., 20
Ulnik, J., 40
unconscious(ness), xvi–xvii, xx, xxii, xxvii, 9, 20, 23, 35, 66, 69, 86, 97, 127, 134 *see also*: conscious
  affecting, 73
  aspects, xvii, xxvii, 134
  association, 82
  assumptions, 134
  attitude, 106
  collective, x, xvi, xviii, xxvii, 82, 85, 90, 135
  cultural, xviii
  dimension, 86
  dynamics, ix, xix
  elements, xxvii
  fantasy, x
  group, 27
  human, 116
  impact, 137
  individual, 20
  issues, 93
  knowledge, 85
  level, 53
  life, xii
  material, 23, 27
  meanings, x, 53–54, 106
  mental processes, x
  mind, xi, xiv
  personal, 93
  phantasy, x
  processes, 59
  social, xii, xiv, xvi–xix, xxii, xxvii, 13, 19–20, 39, 42–44, 53–54, 56, 59, 64, 67, 72–73, 75, 81, 84, 86–87, 91–93, 105, 120, 122, 128, 134–135
Uther, H. J., 100

Vasterling, J. J., 138
Volkan, V., 54

Wardi, D., 92
Warner, M., 106
Weinberg, H., xii, xvii–xix, 1, 13, 15, 20, 23, 37, 39, 44, 54, 56, 67, 73, 83, 86, 91, 120, 134
Weiss, M., xxvi, 55
Wessely, S., 139
Wilke, G., 92
Willoughby, L. A., 9
Winnicott, D. W., xxii, 8, 23
Wolfenstein, M., 11

Yair, G., 71
Yalom, I. D., 50, 53
Yigael, Y., xviii–xix, xxii, xxiv–xxv, 22, 137

Ziaul, H., 140
Zipes, J., xix, 65–66, 69–71, 138–139
Zoran, R., 91